Mindfulness Unlocked

How to unlock your mind to a new and powerful way of life

by Francis O' Toole

To those who embark on a journey of enlightenment

Text of book: © Francis O' Toole, 2020.

Cover photograph: Francis O' Toole, Laytown Beach, Laytown, Co. Meath. Photographer: Jimmy Weldon.

Book cover design: © Caoimhe Mulroy, Once Upon Design. www.onceupondesign.ie

Book editor: Fiona Ashe, FlasheForward Communications. www.flasheforward.ie

Publisher: Francis O' Toole, Slane, Co, Meath. Email: francismartinotoole@gmail.com

Contents

Acknowledgements

Family and Friends

Mindfulness Unlocked by Francis O' Toole

Author's Biography

Francis O' Toole is a teacher, guidance counsellor, career coach and psychotherapist who works with adults and young people.

During his studies in the early eighties in Philosophy and Theology, he was introduced to the concept of meditation and self awareness. He completed a course in Mindfulness-based Stress Reduction with Dave Potter (USA) as his mentor.

After the success of his first book '*Walking On Air — How to face challenges with resilience and adversity with strength*', he continued on a journey of mindfulness. He incorporates mindfulness into his personal and working life practices. He does this through reflection, journaling, meditation and keeping constant awareness of staying in the present moment.

In his psychotherapy practice, he invites his counselling clients to embrace mindfulness as a way of life.

He provides training in mindfulness for individuals and groups, including guidance counsellors, doctors, CEOs of large companies, psychotherapists, international sports stars, teachers, parents, college and secondary school students.

Endorsements of *'Mindfulness Unlocked'*

"Francis O'Toole draws on his experience as a teacher, guidance counsellor, career coach and psychotherapist working with adults and young people to explore and explain, in a very easy-to-understand manner, multiple themes relating to mindfulness. This is a must-read for anyone seeking to find inner peace."
— Noel Dundon, Deputy Editor, Tipperary Star newspaper.

"This practical book will help us to flourish! It can transform our thinking and our understanding of the power of NOW in our lives. A must-have manual enabling us to understand and exercise mindfulness practices that will help us to move rapidly into a more peaceful existence where we breathe a lighter air. The journey to mindfulness can be challenging but Francis O'Toole uses simple language, a clear writing style, incisive explanations and practical tools such as an easy question-and-answer format to guide us to a place of authentic happiness and learned optimism in our daily lives. This book can offer more joy, right now, as we allow Francis to assist us to tap into our inner resources, using mindful reflection, taking time to be in the moment, opening our minds to planning our way to a joyful and fulfilling life!"
— Betty McLaughlin,
Former President of the Institute of Guidance Counsellors,
Wellbeing Team Leader 2016–2019 Junior Cycle.

"'Mindfulness Unlocked' by Francis O'Toole is simultaneously an intuitive and user-friendly introduction to mindfulness, in addition to serving as a relaxing refresher to long-established fans of this approach. Over mid-term break, I thoroughly enjoyed reading this book on a flight home from the States. I loved how the Oracle stories were interwoven with bite-sized gems about how to inject Mindfulness into our daily lives. The personal courage exhibited by Francis, including his own personal experience around the benefits of using a Mindfulness approach, added a storytelling element to the book which kept me engaged throughout. It is not easy to share the private parts of ourselves with a critical and sometimes unkind public.

"As President of the Institute of Guidance Counsellors, I am very grateful and proud that one of my colleagues has produced such a positive and valuable resource that can be used by all of our members working with learners across the lifespan. We recognise that no one approach or technique is a panacea for the broad range of issues we address in our daily work and mobilise ourselves continuously to upskill in a diverse range of techniques and theories. However, this timeless little gem is a valuable addition to our toolkit and will help many individuals to combat anxiety, to ground themselves in the present and most importantly to remember to breathe!"
— Beatrice Dooley, President, Institute of Guidance Counsellors.

"When life gets tricky, we all need a wise voice. In these pages, Francis weaves stories of kindness, strength, warmth and wisdom, with teachings of simple mindfulness practices."
— Dr. Brian McClean, Clinical Psychologist.

Mindfulness Unlocked by Francis O' Toole

Introduction

"It is not what you do occasionally, but what you do every day that is important." — Dalai Lama

The alarm rings, I awake and find my mind busy before I embark on a day of activities. I am aware that my body is full of emotions and feelings. Some are beyond my control. *"How will I get through the day?"* I ask myself.

Does the above paragraph sound familiar? We all have become busy in our daily life, so much so, that we find it difficult to switch off and find time for ourselves. I often feel that there are not enough hours in the day to complete all my tasks. This leaves me feeling under pressure. The result of such panicked thinking leaves me feeling tired, exhausted and stressed. When I become stressed or overworked, the result is going to be a poor night's sleep. I go to a little resting place during the day but I still find my mind too busy and I am unable to switch off.

I have often expressed my feelings of frustration and anxiety with friends and colleagues. I become even more stressed when they say things like *"slow down"* or *"take a deep breath"* or *"take time out of your busy work life."* In the back of my mind, thoughts are saying, *"Yeah, right — easy for you to talk."* Yet, if I am to be totally honest with myself, they are right. The universe gives us the same equal time but how we choose to use it is up to ourselves.

Did you ever find yourself spending the weekend catching up on work or find yourself on a break and planning your next move? Throughout my life, I have worked on time management skills and planning short-term and long-term goals. I keep on thinking I am in control but deep down I find stress and anxiety lurking in the background. I would be the first to admit that a certain amount of stress is good for me. We need stress to help us to respond to any situation. Our reaction could be fight or flight. We have developed this from evolution. It is part of our survival instinct. We may be fighting internal or external messages that trigger the brain in a certain way. Hence, stress is good but prolonged stress is not healthy. It will affect our sleeping habits, concentration, ability and it will affect our memory. All of this causes lasting damage to our body, mind and spirit.

From my experience as a teacher in the secondary school system I have seen a rise in the levels of stress among teenagers. Irish society is full of teens suffering from stress at work or in school and college environments. Some will be lucky enough to attend their school/college counsellor and talk about their issues while others will be referred to a Child Adult Mental Health Service (CAMHS) psychiatrist who may, after consultation, prescribe medication.

Anxiety is one of the main issues facing young adults who are seeking help for mental health issues. This is according to research published in the Irish Journal of Psychological Medicine, 2017. The Children's Ombudsman demanded more support for young people. A study carried out by the National Suicide Research Foundation in 2017 of 1,000 young children with an average age of thirteen found 14% of teenagers had depressive symptoms, 24% had anxiety and up to 20% had attempted self-harm (Larissa Nolan, The Irish Times).

It is a common belief that 70% of people will create a dependency on medically-prescribed drugs, whereas 70%

Mindfulness Unlocked by Francis O' Toole

of people who embark on counselling or mindfulness for anxiety will recover and learn to deal with their issues. One of the most astonishing facts I discovered when researching mindfulness meditation is that scientists can now prove it has a profoundly positive effect on the brain. Mark Williams in his book *Mindfulness* tells us, *"Recent scientific advances allow us to see the parts of the brain associated with such positive emotions as happiness, empathy and compassion. They become stronger and more active as people meditate."*

I often say to students in school, *"Life is simple, don't complicate it."* After working in the caring profession since 1988 — as a psychotherapist, teacher, career coach and now working with mindfulness — I believe stress and anxiety can be dealt with without medication. I believe mindfulness is a viable answer for all of us working in busy environments and responding to the daily pressures of modern day life.

This book will help the busy person under pressure who wants to manage time better and deal with stress. I believe that mindfulness can help to address some of the more common problems that our busy lives lead to. Over the years as a therapist, clients have shared with me issues ranging from stress, tiredness, burnout, physical aches, pains, anxiety and depression. I believe these types of problems are common to most people, especially those who live busy lives.

This book will introduce you to the life-changing practice of mindfulness, helping you to destress, find your own unique space of calm and ready yourself for whatever challenges (good or bad) your busy life will bring you. We all have a rich pool of strength deep within us; we just need to tap into this amazing resource. Through mindfulness, you will become more efficient and effective and make the most out of the time given to you in your situation. I have learnt through mindfulness the ability to manage my stress at home and in the working environment with ease and efficiency.

I invite you to join me on a journey of self discovery using mindfulness, remembering nothing is set in stone as we all need to be realistic in our actions and thoughts.

This poem *Begin* is a philosophical reflection on starting something new again and again — the poem describes a morning walk along the Grand Canal in Dublin. For me, rituals help to slow me down and find happiness in the smallest things in life.

Begin

Begin again to the summoning birds
to the sight of the light at the window,
begin to the roar of morning traffic
all along Pembroke Road.
Every beginning is a promise
born in light and dying in dark,
determination and exaltation of springtime
flowering the way to work.
Begin to the pageant of queuing girls,
the arrogant loneliness of swans in the canal
bridges linking the past and future,
old friends passing though with us still.
Begin to the loneliness that cannot end
since it perhaps is what makes us begin,

begin to wonder at unknown faces
at crying birds in the sudden rain
at branches stark in the willing sunlight
at seagulls foraging for bread
at couples sharing a sunny secret
alone together while making good.
Though we live in a world that dreams of ending
that always seems about to give in
something that will not acknowledge conclusion
insists that we forever begin.

— *The Essential Brendan Kennelly.*

Mindfulness Unlocked by Francis O' Toole

Reflection Questions

"You can't stop the waves, but you can learn to surf."
— Jon Kabat-Zinn

I often compare mindfulness to garden work. I have to prepare the ground, plant seeds, water and nourish the plants, then wait patiently for the results.

The following questions have helped me focus on my understanding of mindfulness:

1. What attracted me to mindfulness?

2. What do I hope to get out of practising mindfulness?

3. What difficulties may come up and prevent me from getting the best from myself on this journey?

4. Am I able to create an awareness of my feelings?

5. When will I practise and at what time?

6. Where am I planning to practise (e.g. bedroom, sitting room, home or at work etc.)?

I found it really important to set time aside — ranging from five to twenty minutes daily — to practise exercises in mindfulness. The most important thing is to practise in a quiet place, turn off the phone, and make sure I cannot be disturbed by others.

Mindfulness Unlocked by Francis O' Toole

1. Mindfulness Will Enhance Your Life

"The way to right wrongs is to turn the light of truth upon them." — Ida B. Wells-Barnett

I know mindfulness is not a miracle cure for all problems or sickness that I have experienced. It is not a replacement for the medical profession or a replacement if I need to take prescribed medication. But the practice of mindfulness has given me strength to deal with trauma and disturbing events with dignity.

I've found that mindfulness helps:

- to improve my motivation and energy levels;

- to improve cognitive ability skills and improve my wellbeing;

- to feel happier and more content;

- to be more productive and effective;

- to boost my immune system and improve my general health;

- to improve my memory and concentration and increase my brainwave activity;

- to enhance my imagination and creativity;

- to create a more enjoyable, meaningful and fulfilling life;

- to decrease my stress levels and boost mental health;

- to face challenges with resilience and adversity with strength.

Mindfulness Unlocked by Francis O' Toole

2. Daily Practise and Journal Work

"It's about living your life as if it really mattered, moment by moment by moment by moment."
— Jon Kabat-Zinn

I find it important to practise mindfulness daily, to notice how it is having an impact on my life. Mindfulness has allowed me to become more aware, tuning into the present moment rather than looking to the past or trying to predict the future.

I also found that keeping a journal is important: writing daily reflections has allowed me to gain insight into my actions. When writing in my journal, I try to be as honest as possible, sharing my deepest thoughts and vulnerable self in a non-judgemental way.

I may write about a dream I had while asleep or about an interesting person I met during the day or I may write about daily short term and long term goals. I certainly find journal writing rewarding and refreshing. It helps me to have mindful awareness of all my actions, where I am fully alert and present in the moment.

I find this experience cathartic, allowing for self-healing in a therapeutic way. Some days I only write a word or paragraph; if I feel really reflective I would write a full page. This kind of awareness in the present moment has resulted in stress reduction.

I gained insight into my personal self by evaluating my actions and reactions, then allowing for change where necessary. Last December I brought my car to be serviced before going for the NCT test — the car failed the NCT test. I became angry and annoyed with the people who did the car service and the people responsible for the NCT test. When I became aware of my anger, I took deep breaths and went for a walk to calm down. I could see that I can be easily triggered if things do not work out as planned. On reflection, I had to learn to accept that the car had a major problem and the right response for me was to take action, control my feelings and go get the car sorted out.

The insight gained for me was huge — an action happened and I reacted. Now I know when an action takes place, I need to reflect and then respond to the situation.

The result of my journal work is fulfilling, allowing for personal growth and a greater understanding of who I am when focusing on my wellbeing, mind and spirit.

When I read back on my journal work, I can see the times when I was struggling with this whole concept of mindfulness. There are days when it made great sense, especially when life seemed to be going well. But there are times when I find it difficult when life offered new challenges — to be honest, there were moments when I felt like giving up on the idea. That is why I need structure and a framework when practising mindfulness. I found it really important to practise skills in mindfulness daily. It is only through daily practice that I am now able to use mindfulness effectively and with ease.

I will try to bring mindful awareness to a 'routine' activity and be totally present in the moment — like washing the dishes, waiting in line at the ATM machine, sitting in a boring meeting, walking from the car to my office, or brushing my teeth.

Mindfulness Unlocked by Francis O' Toole

Before I go to bed each night, I will recall at least one example of simple 'mindful awareness' I had during the day. *"The life that is not examined is not worth living."* — Plato.

I invite you to write down something positive that happened today. Then write about how reflecting on your experience allowed you to gain a greater understanding of mindful awareness.

Mindfulness Unlocked by Francis O' Toole

3. Oracle Rhema

"The real meditation is how you live your life."
— Jon Kabat-Zinn

In Ancient Greek times, the people believed an Oracle was a person who was inspired by the Divine. They could provide great wisdom and insight into any situation. The priest or priestess would claim to be an Oracle touched with a divine call and would speak the words of the gods. The Oracle was seen as a portal through which the gods would reveal their message to the people. When kings, citizens, politicians and philosophers were seeking answers to the big questions in life, they would come to the Oracle for guidance on issues of government policy, war, duty, family life and even personal issues.

This belief was also found in other world religions, for example: Christianity, Buddhism, Judaism, Hinduism and the Egyptians. Even in Ireland before Christianity 400 BC, the Celtic people had a flourishing spiritual tradition with druids who were seen as the Oracle. The followers of Celtic tradition also believed an Oracle could be a sacred place where you could contact the gods and experience their presence. For thousands of years the Celts valued all of nature, believing divinity is around them; in the hills, trees, animals, rivers, sea and sky.

While mindfulness is not a religion or belief system focusing on the Divine or gods, it embraces who we are and respects the culture and religious beliefs of people. It is for this reason I chose the title for this book *Mindfulness Unlocked* — it is an invitation to release the power of your mind.

I use the Oracle Rhema to reveal great stories of wisdom and insights gained from practising mindfulness. I choose the Oracle Rhema as a powerful and graceful woman because of the many contributions women continue to make in our society. The word Rhema is used by two ancient Greek philosophers, Plato and Aristotle. The name Rhema in Greek means something that is spoken clearly and vividly, revealing an important message.

The Oracle Rhema is found in many of my stories, giving us teachings and an understanding of what mindfulness is. She travels to different places and countries, places where I had a positive experience — this is to highlight that she is not confined to one place or time. On her travels, she interacts with lots of different groups and individuals, spending time sharing experiences.

I believe stories capture us and grab a hold of our imagination, always revealing a message. These stories will command attention and create an impact calling us to take positive action which is far greater than any teachings; they will help us to put mindfulness into the context of our daily experience, giving us a new philosophy for living.

While the Oracle Rhema will reveal a philosophical approach to mindfulness, she will also remind us of how we can learn from the greatness of those who have gone before us. The Oracle Rhema explains how 'self-mastery' can improve our life; to quote the words of Leonardo da Vinci, *"One can have no smaller or greater mastery than mastery of oneself."*

Mindfulness Unlocked by Francis O' Toole

4. The Body Scan

"I cherish my own freedom clearly, but I care even more for your freedom." — Nelson Mandela, 1991.

I went to an all-boys primary and secondary school in Templemore, Co. Tipperary where there was a lot of emphasis placed on promoting sports. When I was in first year, the school won their first All-Ireland senior title in hurling. The school had to wait 39 years up to 2017 to win their second All-Ireland. The boys on the team were proud to wear the school jersey and I looked up to them as my heroes. They gave me a new thinking — a healthy body will produce a healthy mind. Throughout my life, I continued with daily physical exercise and enjoyed many aspects of sports ranging from boxing, swimming, water sports and team sports. As I get older I am down to jogging and lots of walking. Finally, I find a good excuse to simply lie down and do nothing! The body scan is about relaxing the body but it is also about becoming aware of the sensations in different parts of the body from the head, back and down into my feet.

The body scan is a major exercise associated with mindfulness training. It helped me learn to focus my attention on different parts of the body. This helps me to anchor my awareness in the present moment and gives me the experience of deliberately and intentionally placing my attention there. I need to be curious about how my body is from day to day and observing any sensations that I become aware of.

It is important to do the body scan in my own time when relaxed and be aware of personal limitations. I really enjoy this exercise. It can be reaffirming after a long day at work or just when I need time to myself.

I invite you to try the body scan. This exercise could last from five to twenty minutes, depending on the time you have available.

Preparation for the Body Scan — you will need:

- a comfortable warm place to lie down on the floor. If this is not convenient it can be done seated;

- a blanket to cover your body can be used to keep you warm (optional);

- a quiet place and make sure to switch off phones.

- Then focus on noticing your body and bringing awareness to sensations as they arise.

Sit in a chair or lie on the floor. Be as comfortable as possible. Gently close your eyes and become aware of your breathing. Take your time. Become aware of your in breath and your out breath. When you become aware of any tensions, breathe into the tension and visualise it leaving your body on the out breath.

We are now going to bring our awareness to the physical sensations of our body.

Begin with the head. Become aware of the sensations: are you tired or alert? We are allowing the mind to become calm and be in the present moment.

Moving the awareness to the different parts of the body: the neck, shoulders, back, chest area, down to the legs and feet. When you go systematically through each part of the

Mindfulness Unlocked by Francis O' Toole

body, you are placing that part of the body at the centre of your focus allowing it to relax and just be.

Go through each part of the body as slowly as possible. Become aware of your breathing into each part of your body, renewing and bringing new energy.

When you have slowly gone through the whole body, then imagine a bright light in the breath which is going to every part of the body. This bright light is bringing healing, life and energy.

As you come to the end of the body scan, become aware of your breath and take five deep breaths before opening your eyes.

I find the mindfulness body scan very helpful to focus on different parts of the body and their sensations rather than being trapped in my mind always thinking. This exercise has certainly helped me to reduce stress and anxiety, allowing for greater calmness in my life. I do the body scan exercise at least three times a week. This helps me to monitor my body and mind, making sure I find time for resting and self care. There were times when I fell asleep during the body scan; in the beginning I would be frustrated by this. Now I accept that I may be sleepy and tired. I try to catch myself when feeling sleepy and focus attention on the breath to help keep me awake.

When I have finished the body scan, I can go back to my daily life with a renewed sense of awareness of perceptions and energy.

Mindfulness Unlocked by Francis O' Toole

5. Meditation

"Surrender to what is. Let go to what was.
Have faith in what will be."
— Sonia Ricotti

A couple was in deep conversation while strolling through the City of Seville in Spain, which is widely regarded as the home of classical flamenco dancing and also the resting place of Christopher Columbus (1451–1506) the famous European explorer. He completed four voyages across the Atlantic and led the first European expeditions to the Caribbean, Central America and South America. The couple was wondering whether there were areas that still needed to be explored. They came across the Oracle Rhema in deep meditation. They were impressed with her pose of statue-like stillness, giving the impression she was at total peace.

The man wanted to rush over to speak with the Oracle Rhema but the woman suggested they sit patiently in silence and wait until the Oracle Rhema was ready to speak.

After a long time the Oracle Rhema began to move and went over to the flowers she had been staring at. Then the couple asked the Oracle Rhema, *"What are you thinking while meditating?"* to which the Oracle Rhema responded, *"Look at this rose."* She held the rose by the stem with her fingers, laying the rose gently on her hand. The Oracle Rhema said to the couple, *"How can you ignore such beauty? Look at its delicacy, taking in all the colours and even watching how the colours can radiate when the sun shines on the petals, making them glow."*

The Oracle Rhema finished by saying, *"Real beauty can only be captured in stillness and silence when we approach it with awe and wonder."*

She then gently let go of the flower back to the garden.

I embarked on an academic journey of study of philosophy and theology at the age of seventeen; during my first week I was introduced to meditation. I studied and researched the different styles of meditation and was influenced by the writings of Anthony de Mello (1931–1987), an Indian Jesuit priest and psychotherapist. De Mello wrote several books on spirituality and meditation. He was my role model when it came to meditation and having awareness in the present moment.

Mindfulness meditation awareness invites me to spend time with nature to allow my mind, body and spirit escape from the busy world. It allows me precious time for renewal and re-energising by giving me quality time to relax. Meditation is an essential part of my life; where possible I would combine meditation with nature. For me, there is a relationship between them. Nature is a support for my meditation and meditation can be a support in how I have awareness of nature. When I am in meditation or having awareness of nature, I leave behind the concerns, stress, anxiety, work plans of my daily life. Meditation and awareness of nature allows me to become present to the moment. My body, mind and spirit relaxes — this gives time for renewal of my being. It opens the door of my mind to explore a new vision and allow my emotions to be open to love, compassion and empathy.

The first lesson I had on meditation was to sit on the floor for five minutes and become aware of my breath. Become aware of the in breath and become aware of the out breath.

In the beginning, I found this boring and became self-conscious of others looking at me and their possible judgements. My mind would jump from one thought to another; I was not able to stay focused on the act of breathing just for five minutes. In reality, I was not ready for this; my mind and spirit were not in shape for such a task. But I persisted and, after a few weeks of practice, I was able to find my breath easily and stay with it. By placing the mind on my breath, I am practising mindfulness. I am also strengthening the mind by getting it to focus on one thing only. I am at peace because I am not thinking about other things.

Thus began my journey of mindfulness meditation awareness of breath.

Another meditation exercise I do regularly after I create awareness of breath is to focus on an object in the room — I keep my eyes fixed on the object. This helps me not to be distracted by my thoughts. When I become aware that I am thinking of other issues, I come back to awareness of breath and awareness of the object in front of me. This is mindfulness meditation.

In some sessions while in meditation, I bring to mind a mantra. I will repeat that same mantra over and over e.g. on the in breath *"I inhale goodness and positive energy"* on the out breath *"I release the negative toxins in my body"*. While I stay focused on the mantra, I am practising mindfulness meditation.

I also use Spotify or other apps which can be downloaded free of charge on my phone for a guided mindfulness meditation journey. While listening, I am guided to relax my mind and body.

I will find twenty minutes daily session to meditate. When life is busy and I am under pressure from other demands, then I strive to meditate for two sessions on this day. Two ten-minute sessions or even five-minute sessions I find is really beneficial.

Setting the right atmosphere for meditation is really important.

I always set a timer when I sit to meditate, then I know the length of time it's going to take and I am not there guessing whether the time is up or not. I light a candle. I see this as an important ritual. For me, a candle illuminates darkness, it connects my inner stillness and even connects me with all people who are striving for peace. I then light up the incense — it symbolises an offering of my intention. The scent also opens the pores of my skin to a new freshness. I sit on a meditation cushion with my legs crossed and my back as straight as possible while my hands lay gently on my knees with the palms of my hands open. Finally, I will always mark the beginning and end of a session with the sound of a gong. This structure helps me to be focused and brings me into the present moment. Mindfulness meditation brings me contentment, peace and strength of mind.

I invite you to spend time this week — five minutes daily — in mindful awareness of your breath. I would also encourage you to find some time and space to be with nature: this could be walking the local fields, in a forest or walking by the bank of a river.

Take a flower in your hand and admire its colour and beauty. Looking carefully at the flower, observe its delicate nature and smell the incredible fragrance coming from it. It's really awe-inspiring to think something so

Mindfulness Unlocked by Francis O' Toole

fragile can be so beautiful. By allowing ourselves to see the beauty of nature, it will enable us to see the beauty in all people we meet.

I have often gone on monthly retreats and exotic holidays as a way to seek total relaxation but I keep coming back to nature to find the ultimate way to relax. I go to the beach, sit on the golden sand and watch the waves building up to great heights before crashing on the dry land. I listen with an open heart and ears to the sound of seagulls hovering over the wild waves. The sound created is like an orchestra of nature wanting to touch my spirit. The salt taste lodging on my lips from the sea air awakens my sense of taste and opens my nostrils to the smell of seaweed. I enjoy watching the surfers riding the waves while children build sandcastles, taking breaks waiting for the wind to change to launch their kites. I usually complete the day by taking off my shoes and socks to walk barefoot on the shoreline. Here I complete my 10,000 steps, allowing awareness of my breath and looking at the seashells sparkling like the stars at night.

Having awareness with nature and the meditation of my breath has allowed me to explore my mind and fully engage in the present moment. I know the more I exercise mindfulness the easier it becomes. I aspire to engage daily with mindfulness because it brings me contentment, satisfaction and joy.

Mindfulness Unlocked by Francis O' Toole

6. Mindfulness Morning

"Time flies. It's up to you to be the navigator."
— Robert Orben

Most mornings, I arise before dawn, light a candle and give thanks for the gift of a new day. I know I am now part of an early ancient ritual of welcoming a new day with excitement and anticipation. I will spend time in mediation followed by a short time doing yoga before heading out on my morning run.

Mindfulness helps me to be focused and motivated. I go for a run each day with a smile on my face, full of gratitude knowing I have another day to live to the best of my potential. I would be the first to admit it is not easy to get out of bed on a cold, wet morning. I know I have attachments that prevent me from seeing the world as it is. I get an attachment to the comfort of the bed. I get an attachment to the idea that it is dark outside or it is too cold to run. There is always a danger that I could convince myself that the weather conditions are not suitable and it is best to stay in bed, comforted by my attachments.

It is best to be honest and say I choose not to run in the morning in the dark or I choose not to run if it is cold or wet. It is important that I make the distinction between attachments and what I choose. After all, the weather is in itself what it is but how I choose to look at it depends on my perceptions.

The early morning mindfulness run allows me to make a clear choice: to give in to attachments or face the morning with eagerness. I find myself putting out my jogging gear the night before — this prevents me from giving in to attachments.

Mindfulness allows me to concentrate and prevents me from focusing on attachments. Mindfulness allows me to attend to my thoughts and emotions and allows me to stay present to the moment. When out running I become aware of my legs while concentrating on my breathing — I pay attention to my breath, inhale and exhale. The run is my time to relax and to get away from other activities, plans or concerns. Mindfulness helps my mind not to drift into attachments and a false belief system but to stay focused on the task of running.

When I am out running on a cold wet dark gloomy morning, I allow mindfulness to become my companion.

7. Just Be

"Wherever you are, be there totally."
— Eckhart Tolle

Life is busy for most of us from the moment we wake up in the morning to the time we head to bed at night. I often wonder why we have the need to fill our days with so many activities. There are some who will reach for the phone to read messages or check up on social media before getting out of bed in the morning. There are others who will allow the mind to stress the body by thinking about the list of jobs that have to be completed that day. Even before getting dressed our minds are racing with ideas and tasks to be completed. How many of us will rush out of the house in the morning before having breakfast? How many of us will obsess about what we should wear on the day. How many of us will give our brain the message: *"There is so much to do in such a short time; in fact, there are not enough hours in the day."*

I trained as a First Aid Responder (FAR) with the Red Cross. During this time, I learned the skills required to deliver first aid in the case of a pre-hospital medical emergency. I realised the importance of these skills which can save lives. This was evident especially when I was on duty as an ambulance driver during the Guns 'N' Roses Slane concert in 2017. I was trained for patient assessment, common medical emergency, and cardiopulmonary resuscitation (CPR), which is a lifesaving technique. These techniques are very useful in many emergencies, including heart attack, near drowning or when someone stops breathing or their heart stops immediately.

I also discovered that in the course of a day I will breathe between 17,000 and 30,000 breaths. This means I breathe about 12–20 times per minute. When I exercise or if I am under stress, my breathing increases.

If I manage to slow my breathing right down it will help me to relax, allowing freedom from pain, anxiety and stress, which will help me to live a healthier life having greater awareness in the present moment. The First Aid Responder (FAR) course highlighted for me the importance of breath. The job of the First Aid Responder is to keep people alive and breathing.

I began to have awareness that I took my breathing for granted; I just saw it as something I do automatically. As a result of the training with the Red Cross, I promised myself to live the rest of my life in total mindful awareness of my breathing and to include it as part of my daily meditation.

I discovered that awareness of breath is one of the oldest practices in meditation and for me the simplest.

Strange to think the only thing I have to do at any one time is breathe. Yes, breathe! This is the only single activity that's a must. Yet, it is the one activity I tend to forget to think about; I just do it. I take my breath for granted. Therefore I believe it is so important that we need to be aware of our breathing, to be able to breathe mindfully — 'Just Be'.

To have full breath, I need to do diaphragmatic breathing — or deep breathing — which is breathing that is done by contracting the diaphragm. Deep breaths will allow air to enter into the lungs as the chest rises and the belly expands.

Mindfulness Unlocked by Francis O' Toole

When we are so busy, we tend to breathe from the upper part of our chest, leaving us feeling a shortness of breath.

The difficulty with this is it does not allow our lungs to do their job: to inhale full breaths absorbing all of the oxygen from the air and sending this to the blood which will circulate throughout the entire body, renewing and giving energy to my cells, which are working to keep the body and mind alive.

'Just Be', taking big long deep breaths and sensing my lungs coming fully alive.

I invite you to try the following:

Sit comfortably or stand in a relaxed way.

Bring attention to your breath, imagining that you have a big red balloon in your tummy. Become aware that every time you breathe in, you are inflating the balloon and every time you breathe out, you are deflating the balloon. Observe how your chest will rise with the in breath and fall with the out breath.

This is helping you — 'Just Be'. There will be distractions coming from the outside or your mind will be racing with activity. In a non-judgemental way, allow for the possibility of distractions of the mind — give yourself permission to come back to them later but for now allow your mind to come back to the breath.

You may experience emotions or sense feelings which are natural and part of who you are — allow for this. Once again, no judgements or comments — continue to come back to the breathing. The image of filling the big red balloon in your tummy with the inhale will help keep your focus on this exercise.

We can continue with this breathing exercise as many times as we like during the day. Developing the skill of awareness of breath is crucial to mindfulness. The breathing exercise is one of the first skills taught in the following disciplines: martial arts, acting, sports, singing and teaching. When we focus on our breath, we allow for ourselves: 'Just Be'.

Mindfulness Unlocked by Francis O' Toole

8. Anxiety

"Be happy in the moment, that's enough. Each moment is all we need, not more." — Mother Teresa

A young student came to the Oracle Rhema seeking advice about his high anxiety levels. He was full of anxiety and low-self esteem thinking about all the negative things that happened in his life: loss of a job, breakdown of his relationship, his overuse of alcohol. He was so uncomfortable every time he thought about the future, fear would overwhelm him, creating anxiety — it became a vicious circle of pain.

The Oracle Rhema offered a solution to the young man. She said, *"Having awareness of your high anxiety will allow for honest conversation. It will allow for you to seek professional help. But most of all, remember life's a journey not a destination. Stay in the present moment believing it is through failures that we grow and develop."*

Mindfulness teaches me that I need to be honest and real with myself when dealing with anxiety. There is always the danger that I tend to hide my pain and distract myself by self-medication or going to the doctor looking for medication to treat the problem. I tend to justify my poor behaviour by blaming others. Mindfulness invites me to take full responsibility for my anxiety. This is the first step towards healing.

There is an exercise commonly used by students of mindfulness when experiencing pain and hurt called 'The RAIN Process' by Tara Brach. This distress tolerance skill will help us when we experience anxiety. The acronym

RAIN is an easy tool to remember when practising mindfulness for anxiety.

I invite you to practise the RAIN Process

R — Recognise and embrace the anxiety when it exists.

A — Allow the pain to be there, without trying to control it or pushing it away.

I — Investigate thoughts, stories, feelings or moods the body may experience.

N — Now: this is my experience right 'now' but it's only a part of who I am as a person.

We should try to practise the RAIN Process as much as possible for at least ten minutes daily.

The RAIN Process is like any mindfulness exercise, it will take time to get used to. Dealing with anxiety will demand honesty and direct admission of our vulnerability. We can then move towards self-compassion and self-care, resulting in major changes to our emotions and feelings, allowing us to flourish and reach our full potential. This exercise will certainly help in the process of recovering from anxiety. It is important to work on all the skills of mindfulness found in this book in dealing with anxiety and if the issues persist, attend a counsellor who will listen with kindness and give you more techniques to deal with high anxiety.

Mindfulness Unlocked by Francis O' Toole

9. Darkness

"Fear is a natural reaction to moving closer to the truth." — Pema Chodron

A group of beach walkers came upon the Oracle Rhema meditating early in the morning. They decided to put this question to the Oracle Rhema: *"Why do you get up so early when you could meditate at any time during the day?"* The Oracle Rhema was glad to share her answer. *"I am waiting for the pregnant darkness to give birth to the light, which is my favourite part of the day,"* she replied.

Mindfulness reminds me about the power of silence and the joy I can get by admiring the beauty of nature and the world around me, despite unhappiness or stress. There are times when life can be very difficult and overpowering; I may feel I am in a dark place with no hope of light at the end. These feelings of emptiness can be so real for me when under great stress or very unhappy because life has handed me tremendous burdens to carry such as sickness, unemployment or dealing with a sudden death of a loved one.

Such unplanned events that I have encountered can create a shadow of darkness over my life. My mind will tell me to run, avoid the situation or withdraw; mindfulness is asking me to do the opposite. Mindfulness acknowledges my pain and struggles, challenging me to embrace my burdens of darkness moments. We are challenged to embrace the pain and struggle with love and kindness, while being gently led to the light. I need to believe this is a storm that will pass; there is always light at the end of a tunnel.

I have gone through major unhappiness and stress; I've had dark experiences in my life as a result of sickness, loss of jobs, relationship breakdown, and losing friends and a loved one to sudden death. Each painful moment has the ability to trigger and bring up the pain from other events or experiences. I face my pain and stay with the dark moments, allowing myself to be surrounded by love and the goodness of others bringing me back to the light, believing in hope that all will work out.

To heal the pain I began to spend time with nature: going hiking, taking long walks, hill walking and spending long hours by the sea. There were many moments when I would sit on the sand by the sea and look out at the waves crashing on dry land. Through mindfulness awareness I began to catch 'my mind' going into negativity and darkness. I decided that I cannot change past events or experiences but I can embrace them with love and kindness, allowing me to be open to the light of goodness and hope. I developed the skill of catching myself going into the negative and gently guiding myself into the light of positivity. This experience of going towards the light of goodness is hopeful and renewing. I allow this to touch off all my experience of people, friends, relationships and at work. There may be dark moments in all our lives but we have the power in our minds to choose to sparkle joy, love and kindness.

Summer

It is time,
Summertime.
Wipe away the winter tears.

Mindfulness Unlocked by Francis O' Toole

Waves glow in gentle sun.
Silence and tranquillity
Guided by the gentle hand
Of the unseen.

Look to nature for life,
Rivers bending,
Rocks blending,
Trees rooted.

Mother Nature's delight
Sacred tears
Flowing life vivaciously,
Bestowing grace.

Mindfulness Unlocked by Francis O' Toole

10. Nature

"If we could see a single flower clearly, our whole life would change." — Buddha

The Oracle Rhema was speaking to a group of students about the importance of caring for the environment. She tells a story about herself out walking along the beautiful banks of the river Boyne when a large fish jumped up to catch some flies but landed on the bank of the river. She immediately ran to save the fish but was aghast when the fish began to talk. *"What is this land?"* asked the fish. She responded, *"A land of honey, fruit and plenty of vegetables."* The fish asked her to show him around the land. Gladly she cradled the fish in her arms, showing him the woods, fields and trees with all its fruit. The fish described his world under the water, which is equally filled with such beauty.

The fish and herself became great friends in such a short time. Unfortunately, the fish needed to get back to the water to breathe. The fish asked in his enthusiasm if he could join her on land. She answered, *"Man and animals are created to serve each other, not to live together. But one day plastic will unite both our worlds in destruction as it destroys the environment."*

During the Palaeolithic and Mesolithic age (300,000–5,500 B.C.) humans depended directly on nature to provide for their daily needs; hunting, fishing and gathering of plants was a normal daily activity. The people of this period would use up all of the natural resources they could find locally, then they would travel to new pastures where there was an abundance of new vegetation and animals. There they would set up camp and exploit whatever was available to meet their daily needs for survival. Our ancestors were always on the move looking for new places to explore and survive.

I can only imagine that living conditions must have been challenging, tough and harsh while at the same time offering a lot of adventure. Living in a tent or a cave could not be pretty; probably at that time the only real comfort came from the wrapping of animal fur around their bodies and the warmth of a fire using flint to spark it. The daily routine and journey of any individual was totally determined by nature. It was only around 5,500 B.C. that people began to develop the idea of settling down in one place and making the best of what the local area had to offer; this was the beginning of the process of farming.

To me, the real richness of this period was the ability of humans to connect and live off nature; this was the way life for thousands of years. I tend to look back at this age in a romantic way and suggest people had no stress or anxiety — certainly not in the way we experience both in modern day society where we live lives commuting to work, spending long hours in offices sitting at a computer while worried about finding accommodation or paying mortgages. In comparison, life for our ancestors seems so simple whereas life today is so complicated with the influence of technology, social media and meeting daily deadlines.

However, if I am to be honest, I am delighted to be living in this incredible age of new discovery resulting from advancement in science, technology, engineering, arts and maths.

I believe mindfulness is inviting me to learn from the experience of our ancestors; while not expecting me to go native living as a hunter, mindfulness is inviting me to connect with nature more. Our ancestors lived daily with nature playing a major part, however there are times when I fail to connect with nature.

I can only say that I need to spend more time connecting with nature, putting my phone to one side. It begs the question, *"Why am I working longer hours making more money if I don't have the time to enjoy the simple things in life?"* I have often gone for long walks along the banks of the Boyne river from Slane to Drogheda and passed by the ancient site of Newgrange, reminding me of our ancestors. This site at Newgrange was first established over five thousand years ago. Here I can see the passage tomb built by stone age farmers to celebrate light. The passageway and main chamber were constructed so that they would align with the rising sun at the winter solstice. This has been celebrated by pagans for thousands of years. I was there in the early morning of 21st December 2018 to experience the pagan dance and beating of the drum, welcoming the rising of the sun. I find it comforting walking in this area, knowing that the first migrants to Ireland found shelter and meaning to their life here.

Long walks have a soothing and calming effect on me. The long walks also have a therapeutic effect on my mind, freeing it from anxiety and the stress of work. Spending time with nature can certainly leave me feeling calm, refreshed and happier as a person.

I stop, sit on the grass and watch the beautiful flow of the river Boyne giving life to fish and insects. I watch the tall trees reaching to the skies while noticing how the light shines through the branches and leaves. Connecting with nature allows me to realise I am in touch with the greatness of the universe. Just by being with nature allows me to feel positive and improves my wellbeing.

The following exercise has helped me to mindfully connect with nature.

1. It is so important to let things unfold in their own time. I give myself permission to take time away from the demands of work or social commitments to spend time with nature. I need to learn the ability to disconnect from the phone, social media and computers.

2. When out walking in nature, I focus on my intention for the time I am going to spend in nature. I tell myself this is my time for renewal, to be energised and refreshed.

3. If I am going on a long walk or hiking, it's not about achievement or reaching a destination, it's about enjoying and living in the moment as I take each step.

4. I allow all of my senses to be open to the experience of nature: the smells, the awesome sights, the different sounds of animals, wind and flow of rivers. I eat some fruit and feel the ground beneath my feet while allowing my hands to experience the gift of touch.

5. I now let go of all judgements and enjoy the simple experiences of nature. Allowing my mind to be in a non-striving mode, paying attention to the here and now. I allow the sun to shine gently on my face and experience the gift of life in that moment.

6. I have personal care in how I treat the environment. By reducing consumption and recycling, I help to reduce the costs and environmental burden of waste.

Mindfulness Unlocked by Francis O' Toole

7. I have gone hiking through *'Ireland's Ancient East'* and along the *'Wild Atlantic Way'*. I am inspired by nature, history and discovered a region of legends and stories from ancient times to modern day times. Ireland has so many places for adventure and hiking, allowing me to experience the way of life of our ancestors while connecting with nature at its best.

I now have a mindfulness awareness about the need to care for the environment and I admire all those around the globe who are creating an awareness of the dangers of global-warming. I believe both mindfulness and nature are so connected with each other, they allow our senses to be fully alive in the present.

Mindfulness Unlocked by Francis O' Toole

11. Pilgrims

"We must be willing to let go of the life we have planned,
so as to accept the life that is waiting for us."
— Joseph Campbell

Each year thousands of people gathered for a pilgrimage to climb a mountain that was considered sacred and blessed by the gods. Over time, they had forgotten the reasons their ancestors started this tradition.

The people were unsure what they were seeking but shared their concerns with the Oracle Rhema, *"We always ascend the mountain to follow in the footsteps of our ancestors but now believe it is time for a new way of thinking."*

The Oracle Rhema told the people, *"It is time to obviate the old way and take on a new way."* She then went on to say, *"Why not take a path where no other has gone and leave a trail behind for others to follow?"*

I brought my children on a trip to Mount Pilatus which is overlooking Lucerne in Central Switzerland. Tradition has it that the mountain got its name because Pontius Pilate was buried there. There is also a medieval legend believing that dragons with healing powers were living on the mountain. I wanted my children to share in the awe and wonder of nature, so they would be able to develop their own appreciation of nature.

Mindfulness has allowed me through nature to strive to extirpate negativity from my daily life. This allows for a gargantuan heart of love, joy, compassion, peace and happiness.

Mindfulness Unlocked by Francis O' Toole

12. Starfish

"You cannot control the results, only your actions."
— Allan Lokos

Sunshine and warm weather is just one of the reasons many Americans retire to the beautiful West Palm Beach, Florida. This is certainly a very wealthy part of America, full of expensive shops, golf courses and beautiful beaches. It is here that an elderly man out walking along the white sandy beach encountered the Oracle Rhema with thousands of starfish nearby.

The man was very curious and asked the Oracle Rhema, *"What are you doing?"* The Oracle Rhema responded, *"I am saving the starfish."* The man said, *"That is impossible since there are so many."* The Oracle Rhema threw another starfish into the sea and said, *"Well, at least I saved this one."*

During the festive season of Christmas, I was in Dublin city centre — it was really great to see so many people out having a nice time. Carol singers and musicians were doing a great job in helping to bring the spirit of Christmas to Dublin's Grafton Street while the shoppers were in search of gifts that may appear under the Christmas tree on Christmas Day for their loved ones. There was a large group of young teenagers from Belvedere college collecting money for the homeless. They reminded me of the importance of giving, especially to those in need. According to Focus Ireland, there were 9,753 people homeless in the week of December 24th–30th 2018 across Ireland. The number of homeless families has increased by 15% since December 2017.

More than one in three people in emergency accommodation is a child. On this day, I met a young man begging and feeling the cold; I offered for both of us to go to Bewleys café (established in 1840) for lunch. He smiled and accepted the offer. How easy it is to make another person smile with a small gesture of a random act of kindness. I know the issue of homelessness is a major national problem, but at least I am aware and able to help someone in a small way.

Mindfulness practice gives me the strength of mind and generosity of spirit to have an awareness of those who are living in constant poverty. I strive to help others in whatever way I can. I never give up, even when the task seems impossible.

13. Bees

"In all things of nature there is something of the marvellous." — Aristotle

The Oracle Rhema tells a group of gardeners the zen story of a beekeeper who was asked by his friend, *"Why do you care for the bees, knowing that they will continue to sting you?"* The beekeeper responds, *"It is in my nature to care, it is the bees' nature to sting."* She concluded by saying, *"As a result of this process, the jars of honey will end up on a shop shelf."*

Even if you are not mindful by nature, you can develop good habits to help you lead a more mindful life and, just like the bees, leap the rewards.

I often feel overwhelmed and stressed with the amount of jobs I need to complete in any one day or during the course of the week. My nature was to be more reactive than proactive and I realised this was contributing to my stress levels. To cope with this, every day I write into my journal or place a note on my phone listing the tasks that I have to complete. I then look at the short tasks that must be done immediately and leave everything else to the end. At the end of each day, I look back over my list. I may not have completed everything but have a feel good factor when I cross off my list the work that is done.

Mindfulness reminds me that life can be challenging and demanding, creating lots of personal pressure, but if I persist, the result will be personal growth and achievement.

Mindfulness Unlocked by Francis O' Toole

14. The Challenge

"Each morning we are born again. What we do today is what matters most." — Buddha

Traditionally pilgrims climbed Croagh Patrick on Reek Sunday every year, which is the last Sunday of July. They were loaded down with their rucksacks, sticks and boots to face their challenge, which can be difficult — especially near the top, which is full of rocks and stones. They asked the Oracle Rhema how should they approach the mountain. The Oracle Rhema responded, *"First write a song about the mountain; dance and sing showing your respect for the mountain and acknowledging you are on sacred ground. The spirit of those who went before you will be your guide and keep you safe from your first step to the top."*

The practice of mindfulness gives me strength to face challenges with courage; to take a new approach when faced with difficult challenges if the old way is not working and to see things with a new vision.

I have often found myself faced with challenges as I journey through life. There will even be times when the challenges seem too much and overwhelming, so much so that I could easily give up saying, *"I cannot cope, this is too difficult."* I may even have voluntarily taken on a challenge hoping that it will improve the quality of my life but may find it so difficult and tough that I want to give up. For example, I registered for a part-time postgraduate course in law at Limerick University but gave up because of the pressure and stress it involved.

There are many ways to tackle a challenge. I often think in challenging situations I need to believe in myself and allow for a mindful approach that will allow me to break down the challenge step by step in the same way as I would approach a mountain climb, taking one step at a time. If I take on this new approach — taking one step at a time and always looking for support — then I am capable of facing any challenge. This will allow for the impossible to become possible. I went back to Limerick University and completed a postgraduate course in Information, Communication and Technology (ICT).

Whenever I am faced with a difficult challenge, I first create awareness about the challenge then I embrace it for what it is. I will be mindful of not becoming too stressed about this challenge and keep focus on my mindfulness awareness exercise of taking deep breaths and staying in the present moment. I will use positive language at all times, telling myself, *"This is possible."* I will gather all the information I need about the project and look for support if others are in a position to help. There is an old saying: *"Rome wasn't built in a day"* so I take one step at a time, beginning with baby steps until I gain confidence, continuing to move forward. Whenever I persevere and succeed, my heart sings with joy.

Mindfulness Unlocked by Francis O' Toole

15. Mindful Seeing

"Don't ask what the world needs. Ask what makes you come alive, and go do it. Because what the world needs is people who have come alive." — Howard Thurman

I was very fortunate to visit Monet gardens which are located 80km west of Paris France in the village of Giverny. Monet could look at nature and the world through light and colour, expressing this on canvas. I stood in his garden, walked on the bridge that he painted on canvas so many times, which is overlooking his water lily pond.

This may seem pretty obvious but it's amazing how much I see with my eyes except the amount of detail missed because I take so much for granted.

I have often sat out in my own garden to watch the beauty of the flowers but failed to see and appreciate the uniqueness of each individual flower.

Mindfulness awareness has taught me to go into the garden and look at the flora and fauna. These words are coined by biologists to refer to a collection of plants and animals in a geographical location at a particular time. I don't even have to name them, just focus on their colour and beauty.

I have often sat for ages and just gazed on one flower, taking in its detail, the pure bright colours, its soft velvety petals spraying the air with a magnificent fragrance. A paradise created for the insect willing to explore. This allows me to place my thoughts on hold and get lost in the awe and wonder of nature. I am grateful each time I look at their beauty.

Mindfulness seeing is paying great attention to what I see and blocking out all distractions. This will help to develop concentration and self-awareness. I can have mindfulness seeing when looking at a bird. Observing all the details that can be found: its size, colours, beak, feathers, wings, claws, shape, actions. I am observing the bird as it is and not adding any comments or judgements.

I was inspired by Monet. He must have spent hours and days planning and painting his amazing works of art. Now I try to spend time looking with awe and wonder at the plants and shrubs in my garden. I bring flowers into my home and plant shrubs in the garden. I celebrate what I create and notice how it brings new energy and colour into my life.

Mindfulness seeing allows me to become totally focused and present in a non-judgemental way. I see things as they are, not the way I would like them to be. Mindfulness seeing also allows me to develop the gift of patience. If I develop this gift of patience with nature, I will learn to be non-judgemental and observant. This to me is a great tool that helps me to reduce stress and to be patient with myself. When I look into the mirror, I am more embracing and accepting of the person I see with kind eyes and a kind heart.

I invite you to try the following exercise on mindfulness seeing:

Take an object from the garden or from the room you are in right now and focus on watching it very carefully for a minute or two.

Don't do anything, just keep your focus on the object. Try to stay relaxed; no judgement or comments, just focus on the object.

Mindfulness Unlocked by Francis O' Toole

Look at the object with new eyes as if it is the first time you ever saw it.

Explore every aspect of the object: size, structure, colour, shape.

Allow yourself to connect with the object and show appreciation for what it is.

Mindfulness Unlocked by Francis O' Toole

16. The Eye

"We are what we repeatedly do. Excellence, then, is not an act, but a habit." — Aristotle

The Oracle Rhema was explaining how all parts of the body need to work together to achieve fulfilment. She told her listeners the following zen story.

The eye was describing this beautiful mountain they were standing on with its amazing panoramic view. The ear listened intently but was unable to hear any sounds and said, *"Where is this mountain? I cannot hear it."* Then the nose began to smell intently but was unable to get any scent and said, *"Where is this mountain? I cannot smell it."* The hands tried to touch the mountain and said, *"Where is this mountain? I cannot get my hands around it."* The ear, nose and hands began to talk to each other and concluded the *'eye was suffering from some kind of delusion'*.

Mindfulness invites me to accept things as they are. There is always the danger that I create a new storyline that is way off the truth and creates complications. Acceptance means I am not denying reality. Monet found healing and peace when painting the beauty of flowers in his gardens despite the fact he was suffering from cataracts and lung cancer. He allowed his eyes to see the world as it is without judgement or trying to change it.

I have a room in my house that I see as a healing and resting room. It is decorated as I wanted with colour and plenty of light. The room is often given fresh colour with flowers nicely arranged in a vase. It is here that I find time to read, relax, listen to music and write. My eyes can spot simplicity while engaging the mind, creating a colourful brain full of creativity and imagination.

Mindfulness Unlocked by Francis O' Toole

17. Philosophers

"Many people are alive but they don't touch the miracle of being alive." — Thich Nhat Hanh

The Oracle Rhema was invited to attend a lecture where many notable intellectuals in the area of philosophy were gathered. The purpose of the event was to debate the issues and discuss whether each individual was free to live their life as they pleased. The topics ranged from epistemology to logic, existentialism, freedom, destiny and the universe. The more they argued, the more they exacerbated the problems and were unable to come to a consensus.

After a long and exhausting day, one of the philosophers decided to question the Oracle Rhema and asked, *"Does the soul exist and is it free from Divine influence?"* The Oracle Rhema responded, *"We here agree that the soul is the principle of life; it gives the human feelings, thoughts and personality. Some would say the soul is given by the Divine, others say the soul is created as part of the process of evolution."* The Oracle Rhema went on to say, *"We need to allow our souls to illuminate."* To which a philosopher asked, *"How do we achieve this?"* The Oracle Rhema responded, *"Allow the soul to be free to dance with the rhythm of life."*

Mindfulness allows my mind, body and soul to be 'still', creating awareness and fulfilment in the present moment. This moment of stillness allows me to pause on life, it allows me to slow down, it allows me to explore and really connect with my thinking. I find this difficult to do at times, especially when there are so many demands on my time. Yet, every time I do this, I feel better in myself, re-energised and a feeling of renewal. I get in touch with my soul — the inner me. This allows me to unlock the door of my mind and body, bringing mental clarity and wisdom. It gives me strength to live a calmer life, be more self-assured and be ready to face all the challenges I may encounter from day to day. As Samantha Power once said, *"People who care, act, and refuse to give up may not change the world, but they can change many individual worlds."*

Mindfulness Unlocked by Francis O' Toole

18. Perseverance

"Everything that has a beginning has an ending.
Make your peace with that and all will be well."
— Jack Kornfield

The people gathered to listen to the Oracle Rhema since they loved her storytelling. Each story has a meaning.

On this day, she was asked about the meaning of perseverance. The Oracle Rhema tells them about two frogs who fell into a bowl of milk: *"One frog lost hope and drowned. The second frog kept on kicking his legs with all his might and strength. Eventually, the milk turned into butter and the frog easily jumped out of the bowl."* The Oracle Rhema went on to say, *"Life can be difficult but never give up."*

Mindfulness helps me to build strength within my mind and heart, knowing that anything is possible. If I am willing to persevere, I will get the strength and courage to live life to the full. I like the Japanese idea of the ritual of Sakura: celebrate each day as a new beginning. The fragile blossoms of the Sakura tree are often described as spring snow by Japanese poets. For the Japanese, the cherry blossom has symbolised the rebirth of nature and purity since ancient times. Every time I celebrate new beginnings and have an awareness of my body, spirit and mind, I am allowing my life to blossom like the Sakura tree.

Mindfulness Unlocked by Francis O' Toole

19. Social Worker

"You are the sky, everything else is just the weather."
— Pema Chodron

A social worker made an appointment to see the Oracle Rhema to seek her advice. The social worker shared how anxiety and worry have become a part of her. After working with clients who express daily trauma, she found it difficult to switch off. The social worker wondered if she was doing enough for the clients.

The Oracle Rhema responded, *"Each individual is responsible for their emotions and feelings."* She continued, *"We need to learn to have the ability to stand back, not to feel you have to fix every problem just because you are the carer. Most times we just have to accept a situation for what it is."*

As a psychotherapist I often listen to clients sharing difficulties about their relationships and wanting to fix their partners. An important message I give to them is that they can only control their own emotions and responses to their partner's behaviour.

Mindfulness awareness is reminding us that we are not responsible for the feelings and emotions of others.

I invite you to reflect on the following:
1. Do you ever question are you doing enough for the people you love?
2. As the carer, do you feel you have to fix someone's problems?
3. Is there a situation you may have to accept as it is?

Mindfulness Unlocked by Francis O' Toole

20. Blindness

"Open the window of your mind. Allow the fresh air, new lights and new truths to enter." — Amit Ray

The Oracle Rhema challenged the people from time to time as she travelled across the country. On one such occasion, the people had gathered to hear her words of wisdom. The Oracle Rhema asked them to imagine if they were told they had only six months of sight left before being struck totally blind. I have no doubt that the next six months would be spent searching, exploring and seeing as much as possible. They would make a list of all the people they love and visit them to be able to ensure their image remains in their head. They would visit countries and lands to explore their heritage, traditions and culture.

The Oracle Rhema put these questions to the people;

"What would change in your life if struck blind?"

"Would blindness change the way you live your life?"

"Would blindness force you to give up your job?"

"Would blindness change the quality of your relationships?"

"If we are to be true to ourselves," the Oracle Rhema said, *"We need to observe our thoughts and feelings at this moment."*

She went on to say, *"Would we not be delighted and full of gratitude for the gift of sight? Allow our eyes to see in a new way, look at the artist who uses colours and canvass to create a masterpiece."*

This story allows me to be full of gratitude for the gift of my sight. It also encourages me to think carefully about how I will use the gift of sight today.

21. Letting Go Of Anger

"Life is not complex. We are complex. Life is simple, and the simple thing is the right thing." — Oscar Wilde

The Oracle Rhema was speaking to a group of young people about anger. She began by telling them how bullfighting conjures up a common image of an angry bull charging at the matador's small red cape. *"Yes,"* said one young boy, *"Never wear a red jacket around a bull."* The Oracle Rhema continued, *"Bulls and cattle are colourblind to red. So when the bull moves in anger it is not because of the colour but because of the skill of the matador's movement of the cape."*

Mindfulness encourages me to let go of my anger because hatred will build up in my heart, leaving me carrying unnecessary pain, hurt and disillusionment. When I move in anger, I have lost control within, allowing outside issues to influence my decisions. I need to become the matador in control of my own emotions.

I often look to the game of chess as a guide to life. In chess, I make moves, but must take full responsibility knowing every action has a consequence. It is the same with people and emotions: I need to take full responsibility for how I am feeling and what I am thinking.

I know I would like to take action when angry and I know that it may be a wrong action because I rush in hastily. Most times, when I do things in anger, I regret my actions. I tend to react angrily to negative experiences.

Mindfulness helps me to be more focused. An action takes place, I sit in silence and reflect, allowing the body and mind to calm down. Then when I am ready to respond, I will do so in a more coherent way, leaving me in control of my emotions and feelings.

Earlier in the book I talked about the breath as the anchor of the body. I need to try to practise the breath exercise before making any decision.

I invite you to try the following breath exercise now:

> Become aware of the breath.
>
> Inhale and count 1-2-3-4-5 and exhale 1-2-3-4-5-6-7 (repeat this a number of times).

This simple exercise may last for one minute but it's enough time to allow us to take control of our emotions, feelings and thinking. It prevents us from rushing in and allows time for reflection. Then when we are ready, we will make a graceful decision.

I need to be kind, forgiving and to love myself more. I must live one day of self-discovery at a time.

22. The Real Me

"Mindfulness refers to the awareness that emerges by paying attention, on purpose, non-judgmentally to the present moment." — Jon Kabat Zinn

A woman came to the Oracle Rhema and shared her life story. She said, *"I lived life well, always developing my skills and talents. I qualified from university with a first class honours degree in medicine."* The woman was also delighted to say, *"I never took alcohol or drugs, and physical exercise was part of my daily routine."* The Oracle Rhema praised her for determination, discipline and commitment to hard work in the area of academics. She then went on to say, *"Knowledge will give you power and strength will give you character."*

But she offered her one more challenge: *"Now go and find the real you."* Taken aback by her answer, the woman then asked, *"How can I find the real me?"* to which she responded, *"Reflection will bring you awareness."*

Mindfulness is about living the journey of life with full awareness in every moment, of every second, every hour, day to day. The story of my life is not about achievements or how much wealth I have gathered. When I embarked on this journey of mindfulness, it allowed me through constant reflection to know and understand my true self— *'the real me'* — living, laughing and loving in the present moment.

Mindfulness Unlocked by Francis O' Toole

23. Narcissism

"Nothing is forever except change." — Buddha

A genial student of philosophy — full of excitement and clearly a lover of knowledge — was delighted to be among famous guests who attended a lecture at the university.

He took the courage to ask the Oracle Rhema about the skill in learning wisdom, *"Do we gain wisdom as we learn new knowledge?"*

The Oracle Rhema responded with a question, *"What have you learned so far?"* The young man gladly replied, *"I learned so much from the history of mankind, I hope to gain experience from this knowledge which will help me in the future."* The Oracle Rhema responded, *"Real wisdom is gained by living in the present moment, the here and now."*

Mindfulness has taught me to reflect on the experience of my life. The process of continually reflecting on our life and experience will allow us to be open to learning, making positive changes where necessary.

I am reminded of the Greek mythological figure Narcissus, a beautiful young man who was extraordinarily vain and who fell in love with his reflection in the pool. He was unable to move from his love experience and eventually turned into the daffodil-like flower named after him.

Mindfulness prevents me from getting stuck in past experiences like Narcissus, whose life ended in tragedy.

By having mindful awareness, we will reflect with maturity on the experiences and events of life that will allow for growth and wisdom in the here and now.

24. Mind

*"There is something wonderfully bold and liberating
about saying 'yes' to our entire imperfect and
messy life."* — Tara Brach

A group of scientists and engineers were celebrating their
many achievements in the area of technology and science.
They gathered in the presence of the Oracle Rhema to tell
her how their achievements improved the quality of their
daily lives. They turned to the Oracle Rhema and asked,
*"What else could we do to prove our worth and continue
to receive accolades?"*

The Oracle Rhema first acknowledges their many
contributions to humanity and that, as a result of their
work, society is a better place.

She went on to say, *"The greatest challenge will be to
explore the power of the human mind."*

Mindfulness enables me to understand that my brain
continues to evolve and grow, depending on the
challenges it encounters from day to day. If I choose to
understand my 'mind' then it's time to cultivate
'awareness' of my thinking, behaviour and lifestyle.

There is a zen story told about two men who were found
arguing about their national flag flapping in the wind.

"It's the wind that is really moving,"' stated the first one.
"No, it is the flag that is moving," the second man said
with confidence. *"Neither the flag nor the wind is
moving,"* the Oracle Rhema said, *"It is the Mind that
moves."*

Mindfulness reminds me that I can react differently to my every experience, depending on my opinion.

Whether I have an objective opinion or whether I have a subjective opinion, my conclusion will be different. The mindful mind will develop the skill of gathering as much information as possible, understanding how the difference between objective and subjective opinion can impact on our decision-making process. I look to my wise, mindful mind to have an awareness of the subjective and objective opinions before making any decision.

25. Guilt

"*Looking at beauty in the world is the first step of purifying the mind.*" — Amit Ray

The Oracle Rhema joined with a gathered assembly of young women, who were exploring issues in science, technology, engineering, maths and humanities. This group allowed for an open and honest discussion about the issues of life that were impacting on them. One young woman spoke about some things she had done in her life that she was not proud of, then she asked, "*Is it possible to be rid of guilt and have peace of mind?*" Everyone in the assembly wanted to hear the Oracle Rhema's answer to this question and so listened very carefully.

The Oracle Rhema invited her listeners to visualise the following:

"*Imagine you are walking on the beach and creating deep footprints in the sand; now think of all the negative things you were not happy with during your life. The footprints represent these negative things. A wave comes in and washes away the footprints.*

"*Now you continue to walk on the white sandy beach, creating more footprints; compare them to all the positive things or events in your life. A wave comes in and washes away the footprints.*

"*You continue to walk, creating new footprints in the sand; these footprints will represent all the great and wonderful things; the unknown yet to be experienced.*"

I believe mindfulness provides the key to having peace of mind. As Eckhart Tolle once said, *"You find peace not by rearranging the circumstances of your life, but by realising who you are at the deepest level."*

26. City of Dreams

"Worry is a misuse of the imagination." — Dan Zadra

In February 2019 I got the opportunity to visit Sigmund
Freud's place of work and home in the beautiful city of
Vienna. This is often called the city of dreams because of
Freud's work in the field of psychotherapy and
psychoanalysis. While sitting in the room where he
greeted his patients, I began to ponder on the influence
that Freud's teachings had on my life. I first began
studying his work in 1982 while studying psychology and
philosophy, then in 1994 in Iona College, USA while
studying family therapy and psychotherapy. His insights
into the mind and psychoanalysis is the cornerstone for
my work in psychotherapy. This was an emotional
experience for me knowing that I followed in his footsteps
for over thirty years working in the field of psychotherapy.

I needed time to reflect and think about my experience, so
I headed to the nearest café. I felt very honoured when I
ended up in the famous traditional café central! This café
has a long history since its opening in 1876 and has
become a popular meeting point for leading lights in the
world of art, literature, politics and science such as
Sigmund Freud, Peter Altenberg and Leon Trotsky.

There is so much to see in Vienna, from the Salzburg
Palace, art galleries, concerts, museums or you could go to
discover the best classical concerts. Of course I went to
the Wiener Royal Orchester to listen to the beautiful music
of Mozart and Strauss.

The saddest part of my trip was to the Hofburg Palace,
which dates from the 13th century. A section of this palace
is called the Neue Burg; completed in 1913, it had served

as a speakers' platform. Guests of honour would speak from here and it was the backdrop for public events. But shame and darkness hovers above this spot, since on 15 March 1938 Adolf Hitler gave a speech from here. This a taboo subject. Since the end of Nazi rule in 1945, the only speech given here was by Holocaust survivor and Nobel Peace laureate Elie Wiesel, at the Concert for Austria on 17 June 1992. The doors remain locked. As I stood there, I realised the long-lasting impact words can have either positive or negative. It reminds me of the importance of having mindful awareness of the type of language we use with those around us: at work, in our community or with family.

Mindfulness invites me to have awareness of my present circumstances and observe carefully how my attitude can impact on my feelings, mood and wellbeing. I have thoughts that are created in my mind; these thoughts can be positive or negative. My thoughts can impact on my emotions, likewise my emotions can impact on my thoughts. My mind is interpreting the world around me trying to make sense of it. If my mind sees the world — or my experience within the world — in a positive way, then I feel happy, which will automatically create happy emotions and feelings, leading me to having a good sense of wellbeing. The opposite is also true: if I think negatively, my emotions and feelings will create low self-esteem.

My feelings can also impact on the brain: if I am stressed or nervous about an event, they send a negative thought to the brain, making it think in a negative way. Likewise, the opposite is also true: if my body and emotions feel good and happy or confident, it will send a positive message to my brain.

Mindfulness Unlocked by Francis O'Toole

Mindfulness is inviting me to have constant awareness of the negative and positive patterns in my mind and to understand how my thoughts impact on my emotions. According to Sigmund Freud, I need to have an awareness of the unconscious mind, knowing that it has an impact on a person's attitudes, experiences, mannerisms and thoughts. The ancient Greek philosopher Epictetus (55–135 AD) said *"Men are disturbed not by things, but by the view which they take on them."*

Mindfulness Unlocked by Francis O' Toole

27. Trust

"With our thoughts we make the world." — Buddha

A group of believers gathered to worship for Sunday liturgy, to listen to the Oracle Rhema speak about believing and trusting in God. The Oracle Rhema began with the line: *"There is a story told about a man who had tremendous faith and belief in his God."*

She told a story about a day this man went out hiking and climbed up on a very steep mountain, but then lost his balance and fell a great distance before grabbing onto a ledge. The man — full of faith — cried out to God, *"Oh God, if you are there, save me in this hour of need."* Other hikers came to rescue the man and released some rope: *"Grab the rope and we will pull you up."* The man of faith said, *"No"* then took a deep breath before he cried out aloud, *"I am waiting for God to save me."* A while later he heard the voice of God in his mind saying, *"Let go and I will catch you."* If this was you, what do you think you would do?

Mindfulness encourages me to develop a deep basic *'trust'* in my mind, feelings and emotions. It is crucial for me to *'trust'* my own authority and decision-making ability. In the same way, I need to build *'trust'* in the people within my community. I can make mistakes and make bad decisions but it takes a great person to learn from their failures, which I try to do. It is so important for me to be willing to take responsibility for what I think, feel and for my actions. *'Trusting'* in myself will allow for growth, personal development and a great feeling of wellbeing.

I invite you to reflect on the following questions on trust:

Who do you trust deeply?

How do you build trust in your relationships?

Who trusts you and what does it feel like to be trusted?

28. Gratitude

"When you are in observer mode, just witnessing your thoughts, they lose their power and sting as you begin to realise that you aren't your thoughts. If thoughts were who you are, how would you be able to observe them?"
— Ruby Wax

I was focused on the TV set watching the wedding ceremony of Prince Harry and Meghan Markle in May 2018 in the beautiful St. George's Chapel, Windsor Castle. I was touched by the ceremony, pageantry and glamour. The love the couple have for each other is a great joy and hope for many. I just loved the way Bishop Michael Curry spoke in the homily. He spoke with passion about the gift of love and how love has the ability to change the world for the better. Quoting civil rights leader Martin Luther King: *"We must discover the power of love, the power, the redemptive power of love. And when we discover that, we will be able to make of this old world a new world. We will be able to make men better. Love is the only way. Love can help and heal when nothing else can. There's power in love to lift up and liberate when nothing else will."*

It is said that millions of people worldwide watched the ceremony — this expression of love — on TV. Bishop Michael got so excited in his preaching when talking about love and how it can change our way. He went on to say, *"The power of love has the ability to change the lives of people, change the world as we know it and make this world great for all people, where we will have no wars, famine, or violence and everyone will experience peace, love and joy."* The Bishop has a tremendous inner value system belief about the ideals of love, which were expressed externally that day in the public display of love between Harry and Meghan. There are many stories about the young couple that show them as a symbol of faith, hope and love.

Mindfulness is inviting me to identify my belief system and values; it is challenging me to be strong and to hold on to what is important in my life. My values allow me to have dreams and my goals allow me to be focused. When I remain true to my values and beliefs, there will be a feeling of gratitude. When we are capable of expressing gratitude for the gift of life and the gift of others, we are mirroring gratitude for the gift of ourselves. This will create a good and positive sense of wellbeing.

I invite you to ask yourself the following questions:

> What do I treasure most in life?

> What am I grateful for at the end of each day?

> When or how do I express love when it comes to caring and sharing?

At the end of each day, take a moment to show gratitude for at least one good thing that happened during the day. This feeling of gratitude will create a good feeling of optimism and life satisfaction.

Mindfulness Unlocked by Francis O' Toole

29. A Life Less Ordinary

*"That the birds of worry and care fly over your head,
this you cannot change, but they build nests in your hair,
this you can prevent."* — Chinese Proverbs

The Oracle Rhema continued to tell stories as a way of getting the people of the community to have self respect and respect for others. On this occasion she decided to tell a zen story.

A farmer got so old that he couldn't work in the fields anymore. He would spend his days sitting on the porch observing his son at work. One day the son felt overburdened with his work and was jealous of his Dad sitting in his comfortable chair, watching everything without doing a tap of work.

The son decided that his Dad was of no use anymore because of his old age. So out of total frustration he built a wooden coffin and placed it on the porch. He then shoved the old man into the coffin.

After closing the lid, the son dragged the coffin with all his might to the nearby cliff. Just as he was about to push the coffin over, he heard his Dad calling out. *"Son,"* he said, *"I have one request. Before you push me over, please keep the box with its good timber because your sons might need it in time."*

Mindfulness awareness invites me to treat all people with respect because how I treat others is a reflection of who I am.

I invite you to look at the following questions to reflect on how you treat people within your community.

1. Do I have values of justice?

2. Am I authentic and truthful in my dealings with others?

3. Do I stand up for equality and work to stamp out bullying?

4. Do I reach out to those who are marginalised and alienated from the community?

Mindfulness Unlocked by Francis O' Toole

30. Gifts

*"If we want others to be happy, practise compassion.
If you want to be happy, practise compassion."*
— Eckhart Tolle

A woman came to the Oracle Rhema expressing gratitude for a life of good health, the gift of sight, the gift of speech, use of limbs, touch, smell and memory. The Oracle Rhema looked deeply into the woman's eyes and asked, *"Did you use all of your gifts to the best of your ability?"* She left the woman to ponder on this question.

The Oracle Rhema then said, *"If today was the last day of your life, would your conscience be able to say, 'I used my gifts to help those who were less fortunate than myself'?"*

Mindfulness is inviting me to have awareness in how I use my gifts and talents to improve the quality of my life and the lives of those around me.

I have gifts and talents, but what good are they if I am not willing to share them with others. I often think that we are all chosen to be in this world for a particular reason. I may not understand the reason but if I share my gifts and talents, I may learn to understand more about myself. I need to connect with my talents and have a passion to express them, allowing them to touch my heart and mind. In the same way when I admire the gift of others, it brings happiness to myself. Look at the example of the musicians — they could play their instruments for their personal enjoyment or they could choose to share their gift and play in public, allowing others to be enriched by the sound of music. If I am watching the Olympics on TV or attending a show in the West End London or having coffee with a friend, I allow each of the experiences to have a special place in my heart — I see all of these experiences as a gift to be treasured.

As a teacher of social, personal and health education (SPHE) in a secondary school, I often get the students to repeat the following, *"I am unique and special."* The invitation is for all of us to recognise our own gifts and talents and share them to help make the world a better place. Using my gifts and talents will allow me to grow and develop as a human being.

I invite you to make a list of all of your gifts and talents from communication skills, parenting skills and musical skills to the ability to speak another language. I would encourage you not to hold back but to make that list as long as possible. Celebrate your success. I would also invite you to make a list of the things you could do to make our world a better place using your gifts and talents. There is so much brokenness in the world from children in need, homelessness, illiteracy, neglect of the elderly, etc. Maybe you could choose to do one small thing this week that will bring some comfort to others.

Mindfulness Unlocked by Francis O' Toole

31. Searching

"Your vision will become clear only when you look into your heart. Who looks outside, dreams. Who looks inside, awakens." — Carl Jung

There is a story told about a young postgraduate student who left his home in the pursuit of wisdom, fulfilment and happiness. He first travelled across his own country, greeted and shared experiences with lots of people, but did not find the depth he was looking for. As he became more anxious to seek the truth about the meaning of life, he went further and further from his home, traveling to different countries and stopping and talking to all the people he met on his travels. He would spend time with tradesmen, professionals, teachers and doctors; the young postgraduate student was in awe of their work but still failed to find what he was looking for.

The student eventually came to Belgium seeking wisdom but spent more time eating waffles and chocolate and drinking beer. Then, one day, by accident he came across the Oracle Rhema standing alone, statue-like beside the great Groot-Bijgaarden Castle. Somehow the student could sense there was something different about the Oracle Rhema and decided to sit and talk. The young postgraduate student told the Oracle Rhema, *"I have travelled greatly and met really good people. Yet, I have not found the secret to achieving wisdom, fulfilment and happiness."* The Oracle Rhema gave the young postgraduate student a notebook and fountain pen and told him to visit the castle and return in three hours then the truth would be his. When the young postgraduate student returned, the Oracle Rhema wanted to hear about what he saw before asking, *"Did you see the amazing, beautiful*

garden with all the springs of water within the castle?"
The young postgraduate student was disappointed with
himself that he had missed the spectacular place. The
Oracle Rhema told him to revisit the castle and locate the
beautiful spring garden then come back and the truth
would be revealed.

The young postgraduate student, with total joy in his
heart, rushed to find the garden and came across it in a
very short space of time. After walking around the garden
enjoying the beauty of nature and the way of life of the
people, he then came back to the Oracle Rhema to seek
the truth. The Oracle Rhema asked, *"Where is the
notebook and fountain pen?"* The young man said, *"I was
so busy looking around, I forgot about them and
misplaced them,"* to which the Oracle Rhema responded,
"Enjoy life, but never forget your responsibilities."

This zen story highlights the paramount importance of
understanding that those who live mindful lives have total
awareness of who they are right now and are capable of
taking full responsibility for their actions going forward.
Like the postgraduate student in search of wisdom,
fulfilment and happiness, the mindful person seeks the
same values. In mindfulness I know these values are found
deep in my heart and mind. I just need to live a life of
discovery one day at a time, getting to know myself inside
out.

I invite you to reflect on the following three Rs, which
help me to have mindful awareness:

1. Reflect on all my experience — I ask questions
    beginning with: Who? Why? What? Where? When?
    How? For example, *"What observations did I make?"*
    "Who is involved?" "How do I find a solution?"

2. Record — I make a list of all that happened.

3. Review — I go back over my reflections and records to see if there are implications or if I can make changes that will help improve the quality of my life and the lives of others.

32. Physical and Emotional Pain

"Your present circumstances don't determine where you can go, they merely determine where you start."
— Nido Qubein

Over the last twenty years I was very fortunate to get the opportunity to work in a caring profession as a psychotherapist. This work allowed me to care and share with clients who were trying to understand and struggle with the meaning of their experience of pain in their lives. This often led me on a philosophical journey of existentialism, an approach which emphasises the existence of the right of the individual person to be a free and responsible agent in their life, determining their own development through acts of will. For many, especially those who came for counselling, they had experienced the lack of free will or maybe they had abused their free will, creating destruction. The result in each case was pain and discomfort.

I will never know how I am going to act in any situation until I am faced with the inevitable. If I find myself under too much pressure, I could deny my pain or I might live in denial of my pain deep within or I could misuse substances as a way to distract from the pain. There is a huge difficulty with this: any person under severe mental pressure could submit to the temptation to derive pleasure from drugs and alcohol to avoid facing issues, but their problems still remain. The more a person avoids issues and masks pain with drugs, alcohol or comfort eating, the bigger the problem becomes. This person is likely to become overwhelmed by their problems and continue self-harming.

As a therapist, I get the client to explore and identify the patterns of behaviour which they have chosen. I encourage them to become self-reflective rather than self-destructive. I encourage them to explore all possibilities, working on their pain, allowing for growth and self-determination.

It is never my intention to get the client at any stage to have feelings of guilt or shame resulting from their actions. Nor is it my intention to get the client to a place where they experience more pain and hurt. I do admit I am no miracle worker and I also admit it is not easy for clients to create change, even when they have good intentions. We develop patterns of behaviour over weeks, months and, in some cases, years. Some clients get stuck in a place where they see no light at the end of the tunnel. It is for me as a therapist to reassure them and to get the client to explore ways of dealing with issues and to believe there is always light at the end of the tunnel. This allows for hope, which needs to become part of the new inner belief system of the client.

I believe it is important to develop the strength and courage to identify my pain and brokenness, embracing all without denial. This becomes the starting point for new beginnings and for change. Mindfulness has enabled me to create awareness of my present circumstances. It allows me to explore new ways of doing things. It allows me to embrace the moment while recognising the pain and hurt, believing things can and will improve. I need to learn to feel the sensations and emotions that are causing hurt and pain and not continue to deny the existence of such discomfort. This can have a positive impact as the mind will challenge the body to find new ways of doing things, allowing for more positive patterns of behaviour. In all of this awareness, there are no judgements, labels or self punishment.

Mindfulness Unlocked by Francis O' Toole

There may be times when life seems like a shipwreck but always have hope the lifeboat of our wisdom will bring us to safety. I can easily recall the day I had a near death experience in a surfing accident: as a result of personal damage to my body, there were days when I felt really low which impacted on my self esteem. I fought the pain and never lost hope.

Embracing my pain and coming to a new understanding of my existence allowed for personal growth.

I invite you to reflect on the following exercise:

1. Write down some of the painful moments that are holding you back as a person. Be gentle and kind to yourself as you do this.

2. Write down some of the positive moments in your life: this could be a moment when you smile in the company of a friend.

3. At night recall three good things that happened during the day, this will help you to focus naturally on the positive and also help to give you a good night's sleep.

Mindfulness Unlocked by Francis O' Toole

33. Vote

"Do not let the behavior of others destroy your inner peace." — Dalai Lama

An obstreperous crowd gathered to hear a radical subversive political leader complaining about the Government's odious debts incurred during its term of office.

Those who gathered were getting caught up in the frenzy that was created and began to shout out slogans that were very offensive. Within a short space of time the group turned into an out-of-control mob, using violence and destroying public property.

A discombobulated man turned to the Oracle Rhema demanding to know, *"Why are you not joining in solidarity with the people?"* The Oracle Rhema replied, *"I will wait patiently for elections, then use my power with my vote."*

Mindfulness helps me to understand, reflect and gain wisdom from my experiences.

I believe people have a right to protest, especially when they feel they are unjustly treated. People also have the right to strike if they are looking for better pay and working conditions.

I certainly don't believe that any protest should lead to violence — I strive to be a pacifist. I find it very interesting listening to people daily complaining about Government policy and planning. Yet, I am often amazed that those same people who complain are the very ones who have not voted.

Writing into my journal daily using the following questions as a guide helps me to keep focus and to gain wisdom from my experiences. I invite you to reflect on the following as a guide to gaining wisdom:

1. Do I observe with curiosity my thoughts, feelings and body sensations as the day progresses?

2. Do I acknowledge, recognise and am I aware of my inner resilience?

3. Where have I used wisdom in making a decision or dealing with others?

34. Saying 'Yes' or 'No'

"My heart is open, I allow the Universe to guide me through my thoughts, my intuition, my feelings and my encounters. I am fully open to receive the guidance and to follow it." — Elena Stasik

A young man got the opportunity to study performance arts at a top university. During his studies he achieved many awards and accolades for a number of performances. Now that his studies were completed, he was at a crossroads in life. The young man believed he was destined for great things, with which many of his friends and family concurred. The actor waited and waited for the right opportunity or break that would lead him to his fate of greatness. The actor became impatient with the slow progress of his work, he was saying *'no'* to many shows since he felt they were not the right ones for him.

Impatient and frustrated, he went to the Oracle Rhema seeking advice. The Oracle Rhema's advice was straight to the point: *"Say 'yes' to every opportunity."*

She continued, *"There is no right time to achieve greatness, the time is now to keep saying 'yes' to everything that comes your way. By investing time, energy and experience you will begin to enjoy the journey, realising that the end product is not as important as you imagine."*

Knowing when to say *'yes'* or *'no'* to opportunities can be challenging; there is always a fear that I may say *'no'* to a great opportunity and *'yes'* to a minor moment. Constant mindful awareness will enable me to stop procrastinating and help me to know when it is the right time to say *'yes'* or *'no'*.

I found that saying *'yes'* or *'no'* in a relationship can be difficult. There is always the fear I might get it wrong on this occasion. If my intention is in the right place, then I will be happier with my decision. I know if I say *'no'* to lots of activities or social occasions, the invitations may stop coming my way. Yet, I also know there are times when I need to say *'no'* to distractions in order to be able to focus on my job. Over the years, I have gone back to college as part of my lifelong learning. There were lots of opportunities for a great social life, but I said *'no'* because I wanted a clear head to be able to focus on projects, essays and exams. I found it so important to have clear boundaries. It always worked for me. When I say *'no'*, I am mindful to thank the person for thinking of me and giving me the invitation in the first place.

One year, I got an opportunity to speak at a Novena in Holycross Abbey, Co. Tipperary. I knew that thousands of people descended upon Holycross every year for this solemn Novena. I immediately said *'no'* to the offer. On reflection, I could see fear took over — I questioned my ability to speak at such a large gathering. After sharing my concerns with others, my fear subsided. I then said *'yes'*. The Novena was a great success and I was honoured and privileged to make my presentation.

The following guidelines have helped me to know when best to say *'no'* or *'yes'*:

1. If I say *'no'* to an opportunity, is it because of fear?

2. If I know fear is not the reason for saying *'no'*, what is the reason?

3. Do I have clear personal boundaries or am I afraid to say *'no'*?

Mindfulness Unlocked by Francis O' Toole

35. Mindful Eating

"Mindful eating is a way to become reacquainted with the guidance of our internal nutritionist."
— Jan Chozen Bays

In mindful eating, I pay attention to my food: having an awareness of what I am eating instead of eating mindlessly. I become aware of the food I am eating and asking if this is good for me. This is really promoting respect and care for my body. I am also recognising that I have likes and dislikes but I am careful not to fall into the trap of comfort eating when under pressure.

In recent times, there seems to be an increase in awareness among the general public about eating healthily to protect our body and mind. Eating mindfully is linked to healthy weight and not overeating. Since I began mindful eating, I enjoy and savour my food more and I have developed the skill of self awareness. I now choose to eat the right foods that will be in the best interest of my health and avoid comfort foods where possible.

I know the dangers associated with overconsumption of unhealthy food and drinks. The philosophy of mindful eating is about balance and not denial of food and drinks.

Having awareness through mindful eating allows me to have gratitude for food and an appreciation of those who prepare it. Mindful eating enables me to become aware of the need to make better choices by limiting alcohol, sugar, salt and fat intake.

I may crave food when I am hungry in the same way I crave sleep when tired but if I allow my senses to help in mindful eating, I will approach food using healthy habits.

I know this sounds easy but it can be challenging. I have a sweet tooth and do my best to avoid chocolate and cakes. I could do well for days in saying *'no'* to these sweet foods but could easily end up eating a packet of biscuits watching TV. But each day is a new day and it gives me the opportunity to start again.

I invite you to try the following exercise which is associated with mindful eating and will allow you to use all your senses.

1. Get yourself a raisin or a sweet and sit silently in your chair.

2. To bring yourself into the moment — the 'here and now' — take deep breaths, bringing calm to the body.

3. Take the raisin or sweet and look very closely at it. Look at the colour, shape and smell of the raisin or sweet. Allow your mind to fully focus.

4. Using the gift of touch, attentively and effectively explore every piece of the raisin or sweet, feeling its texture and shape.

5. Using the gift of sight, take the raisin or sweet in your hand. Study it carefully as if it were your first time seeing it. Look at the shape, curves and colour while observing your sense of sight.

6. Using the gift of smell, bring the raisin or sweet up to your nose to get the best smell. Is it evoking any feelings within? Just observe what feelings you have.

7. Using the gift of hearing, bring the raisin or sweet up to your ear and listen for any noise. Can you hear anything?

Mindfulness Unlocked by Francis O' Toole

8. Using the gift of taste, place the raisin or sweet into your mouth. What are you tasting as the clusters of bulbous nerve endings on the tongue engage with the raisin or sweet? What are you sensing? Do you like or dislike it? Don't rush into eating it, remember to keep the raisin or sweet in your mouth for as long as possible. You want to eat it slowly and mindfully.

9. Take a moment or two to reflect on the experience.

   (a) How was it for you?

   (b) Did you gain anything from the exercise?

   (c) Was it different? If so, can you explain why it was so different.

This exercise has helped me to spend longer time enjoying meals and having more chat time with my children and friends. I find myself shopping mindfully for the right foods and I look at the ingredients of foods plus their country of origin. The more I practise the more I will understand it and sense the benefits in my life as it happens moment by moment.

There are a lot of things I can learn from eating mindfully, using all my senses to experience things in a new and fresh way. Each time I am having a meal, I ask myself if I am eating mindfully. Do I use meals as a time of rest and renewal? Do I have the time to sit, rest and really enjoy my food? Am I too busy to taste the food?

Eating mindfully highlights the importance of eating the right foods to nourish my body. Eating mindfully will help me to have self control and self awareness, strengthening my mind to deal with the big issues of life.

Mindfulness Unlocked by Francis O' Toole

36. Acceptance

"Mindfulness is awareness without comment, without discrimination, without judgement."
— Steven Harrison

One of the highlights of my many trips to Switzerland is the Basel Rhine swim. It is a big tradition for locals and tourists to swim or float on the Rhine river from the banks of the Minster down to the lower Rhine banks, which could take fifteen minutes. I was never short of company because daily, especially during the summer time, hundreds of people would be doing this swim. It gave me a new understanding of going with the flow — sometimes I apply this to my life experience.

Whenever I hear the word acceptance, it allows me to be non-judgemental. It allows me to embrace and welcome all things just as they are.

For me, acceptance is not about giving up or about fighting a greater fight. It's about allowing the unfolding of life to be, developing a greater acceptance of how things are.

I know there are so many things in life that I have no control over e.g. death, weather, man's inhumanity to man, famine, war, violence, hatred. I could develop rage and anger and fight every negative issue that comes my way or I could allow the universe to unfold its great mysteries in time.

If I am to act or react to every event and action outside of myself, then I wonder if I am a puppet whose strings are guided by another?

I am challenged to choose living a life of acceptance or going with the flow but rewarded knowing I am not controlling or dictating.

Mindfulness Unlocked by Francis O' Toole

37. Cup of Tea

"The basic root of happiness lies in our minds; outer circumstances are nothing more than adverse or favourable." — Matthieu Ricard

The Oracle Rhema was explaining to her followers that we need to develop open minds if we are to gain insight.

She told her followers the story told about Nan-in, a Japanese master during the Meiji era (1868–1912), who received a university professor into his home who had come to inquire about zen. While sitting at the table sharing knowledge about zen, Nan-in poured tea into the visitor's cup but kept on pouring until the tea was overflowing. *"Just like this cup,"* Nan-in said, *"You are full of your opinions and speculations. How can I show you zen unless you first empty your cup?"*

When I began my postgraduate in education management at the National University Ireland Maynooth, I thought I knew a lot about education. However, the course challenged me to revisit my old way of thinking and it inspired me to look at educational management in a new way. I was encouraged to look at policy, planning and leadership; I realised I had a limited understanding of effective management. I discovered with time, good management in education requires leaders who can be open to new ideas, empathise and bring out the best from their staff and students. If I am to be emptied before I am filled, I need to be open to change and willing to accept the wisdom of others.

Mindfulness is inviting me to be open-minded to new experiences. I have often failed to listen to good advice because I was stubborn. Now I strive to be open to listening to the wisdom of others and I am open to the idea that I am constantly learning.

I invite you to ask yourself: are you able to empty your cup to be open to new experiences?

38. Observant

"It is good to have an end to journey toward; but it is the journey that matters, in the end."
— Ursula K. Le Guin

A group of students gathered to hear what the Oracle Rhema had to say on mindfulness. One student stood up during the talk, saying, *"We have practised mindfulness for two years. Do we get a chance to move to the next level?"*

The Oracle Rhema turned towards the student and asked, *"Did you notice the message written on the big poster outside the door in the entrance hallway?"*

The student was a little puzzled but eventually admitted he didn't even see a poster. To which the Oracle Rhema responded, *"When we have reached the state of observing, then we are ready for the next level."*

I find that life can be so busy that I can lose out on the beauty of simple things as a result of a lack of awareness. I know that I need to slow down and catch my breath in every aspect of my life from family, friends, work, relationships and rest time. On one occasion, I was out on my motorcycle Suzuki 600 driving at top speed from Tipperary to Dublin when a bee got into my helmet visor — this was serious. I had to keep calm, slow down and eventually park the bike safely before releasing the bee. The insight I gained from this experience are good lessons for life:

1. Never panic, play it cool even in a crisis.

2. Be alert and be observant.

3. If I am living in the fast lane of a life full of stress, I can be derailed so easily.

39. Tai Chi

"We are all faced with a series of great opportunities brilliantly disguised as impossible situations."
— Charles R. Swindoll

The Oracle Rhema was explaining the importance of patience to her followers and shared with them the following story of an impatient Tai Chi student to get her message across.

A student of Tai Chi went to his Chinese martial arts instructor and said earnestly, *"I am one of your most dedicated and committed students. How long will it take for me to become a master of Tai Chi?"* His martial arts instructor responded, *"It will take at least ten years of patiently working on all of your skills and strength of mind to become a master."* The eager student was not too pleased with this answer and came up with a new suggestion: *"What if I work longer days and train harder?"* The master replied, *"In that case it will take you at least twenty years."*

I have a little pond located in the back garden of my home, which was full of frogs this year. It left me thinking about the lifespan of a frog. The first stage is the egg stage which are usually laid in or near water. The eggs are laid in large groups and covered in jelly, making them very slippery which protects them from wildlife. The second stage is when the tadpole hatches from the egg. The froglet is the third stage where it grows lungs, legs and a short tail. The adult development is the final stage of the frogs lifespan, when the frog can leave water to live on land.

Tai Chi mindful awareness empowers me to be patient, mentally calm and accept things as they unfold in their own time. Like the cycles of nature, I cannot rush any stage but need to be patient, allowing time, knowing all things will evolve.

40. Stillness

"Seek out a tree and let it teach you stillness."
— Eckhart Tolle

Mindfulness is keeping stillness within when all around you may be full of chaos.

A group of students studying medicine in a major university were curious about the concept of mindfulness. Scientific evidence has recently shown that by practising mindfulness you can reshape your brain and see life in a new positive way, taking on major challenges that once may have seemed impossible.

The students approached the Oracle Rhema to hear her comments on this new scientific discovery. The Oracle Rhema said, *"The Chinese Bamboo Tree lies dormant for four years below ground where it is nurtured, watered and cared for, only to flourish above ground in the fifth year."* She paused to allow the students to assimilate this information.

After a few brief moments the Oracle Rhema continued, *"When we practise mindfulness, do not be surprised if we flourish exponentially over a period of time."*

I am reminded here to develop the skill of stillness and patience, knowing good things will come my way all in good time. Mindfulness is like planting a new seed in my being: the more patient and understanding I am, the greater the benefits. But I need to be patient, persistent and never give up, even when I don't see growth, just like the Chinese Bamboo Tree.

Mindfulness Unlocked by Francis O' Toole

41. Wisdom

"A mind set in its ways is wasted." — Eric Schmidt

The people came to the Oracle Rhema and explained that there were many individuals claiming to be prophets and claiming to have the true message of life.

They asked the Oracle Rhema for advice on whom they should listen to. The Oracle Rhema responded, *"First, trust yourself. Secondly, believe you have the gift of intuition and imagination."*

Mindfulness encourages me to be strong minded, believing and unlocking my inner wisdom. I need to trust my internal compass, the part of the brain that gives me a sense of direction, believing it will guide me on the right path.

I invite you to reflect on the following:

1. Do I allow others to easily influence my thinking?

2. Do I doubt my own views, ideas and insights?

3. Am I true to myself?

42. Dream

"The curious paradox is that when I accept myself just as I am, then I can change." — Carl Rogers

One day the Oracle Rhema described her dream of brokenness with her followers, *"I had a dream, I was in a dark cave all alone, sitting in a corner with nobody around and not a sound to be heard. I began to fear that this was it for me: to die all alone with no words of comfort from anybody or even a hug of love to reassure me that I was going to be okay."* The Oracle Rhema continued, *"There was a message in the dream. It was for me to plant seeds in the ground and watch how they burst into life and blossom with colourful petals."*

The Oracle Rhema then said, *"Likewise with people, we need to find the tribe, group or community where we fit in and belong, knowing we can speak our mind and be accepted for who we are."*

Mindfulness teaches me that if my vision of life is full of negativity then I will find negativity but if my vision is positive, full of love and beauty, then I can expect to find a magnificent world managed by loving people in my community. This is best described in the words of Marcel Proust: *"Let us be grateful to people who make us happy; they are the charming gardeners who make our souls blossom."*

Over the years, I was always part of a community — from parish, IGC counsellors, IACP counsellors, teachers and sports teams. I know I work best when interacting with people. When working, I am a team member who increases productivity and performance — there is an old saying, *"Two heads are better than one"*. But what I gain most when working as a team player is getting to know more about myself — others help me to understand my strengths and weaknesses. I also found that working as a team player can be challenging as others may have a very different worldview than me — this has developed my skills of compromise and negotiation. The greatest thing I have learnt about being part of a community is the friendship, fun, laughter and encouragement gained. A true community will be there to support me and promote creativity. Success is celebrated in the community and in times of despair they will be there to guide, hug, pointing me in the right direction.

I invite you to reflect on your tribe, group or community where you fit in and belong — ask if you can give more to help enhance the group. Maybe you could go out for coffee with a friend from that group and share ideas of how to strengthen the group. Maybe there are areas in your life where you need more support — there is a group out there for everyone. Today is a good day to plant a seed, identify your group.

Mindfulness Unlocked by Francis O' Toole

43. Thinking

"It takes a deep commitment to change and an even deeper commitment to grow." — Ralph Ellison

A woman came to the Oracle Rhema because her mind was so busy, she was always thinking. The woman found it difficult to rest her brain. She told the Oracle Rhema that her mind is constantly thinking and she cannot switch off. The Oracle Rhema reminded her that the average person will have between 60,000 to 90,000 thoughts a day. This is the function of the brain. *"Yes,"* she agreed, *"But how can I control my thoughts?"* The Oracle Rhema responded, *"Stop. Now take a deep breath, breathe in and out slowly."* She went on to explain that, *"The mind is always working but we need to be aware of the messages we send to our mind. Are we sending negative messages or positive messages? With practice we can develop the skill of understanding our mind and getting it to think in a certain way."* She concluded by saying, *"If we think positive thoughts, we have positive feelings in the body and if we think negative thoughts, we will not feel as good."*

I am responsible for my thoughts and feelings. Mindful awareness helps us to understand and have awareness of our feelings and whether our thoughts are negative or positive.

Mindfulness enables me to recognise that my mind is a powerful force which has the ability to elevate or crush my mood because it is always lurking in the background of my emotions. The following list will highlight some of the negative beliefs I may have that affects my mood:

"I'm no good", "I'm a loser", "I'm a failure." Negative thoughts will create low self esteem and lower our energy levels. The same damage is created if I am constantly in a state of worry — look to the advice of Leo Buscaglia: *"Worry never robs tomorrow of its sorrow, it only saps today of its joy."*

Going forward, I know it is okay to think thousands of thoughts daily, but it's really important to have mindful awareness of the impact of my thoughts.

I invite you to ask yourself when having negative thoughts, *"Is there another way I can think about that?"*

Let's try the following mindfulness exercise:

Focus on the image of traffic lights to help you understand your thoughts. If your thoughts are unhelpful — see them as red thoughts. If your thoughts are helpful — see then as them as green. The orange is a reminder that we have the ability to change and to proceed with caution.

The mindful person will try to become aware that if red thoughts are coming into their head, they can choose a green thought instead. This is more positive and more helpful. Some examples of green thoughts: *"I am amazing", "I have great potential", "I love people and people love me."* Life would be so much fun if only we could choose helpful, positive green thoughts. There is an old African proverb: *"If there is no enemy within, no harm can come to you from the outside."* We need to stop building a wall of negativity within.

There is nothing I can do about past events or experiences because they are gone and I can't control the future because it hasn't happened yet. The challenge is to live a life in the present moment, having mindful awareness of my thoughts, and develop the skill of thinking positive thoughts, allowing my mood and senses experience the best of what life has to offer.

I found that thinking poorly about myself brings me down quickly. But when I have positive thoughts it allows me to embrace all moments in my life and reach my full potential. I need to rest my mind from over-thinking. Each time I rest, I find my heart is waiting in silence only to be disturbed by the gentleness of my breath.

44. Storytelling

"A small key opens big doors." — Turkish proverb

One day the Oracle Rhema visited a group of parents where she was greeted with open arms. They wanted to hear whether she had any words of wisdom.

She told them, *"There is always the danger that knowledge can be wasted on the ignorant if they fail through laziness to put their learning into action."*

She went on to say, *"The best gift a parent can give to their children is storytelling. Stories can be used as the key to opening the gift of their imagination and creativity."*

I told stories to each of my children every night before bedtime up to the age of ten. In the beginning, I read and re-read some books. My children liked to hear the same story over and over — it gave them security and they were reassured by the sound of my voice. It is my hope that my children will continue to read stories which will spark their imagination and creativity. As they get older, they are beginning to develop their own personal story with a daily new experience of the world around them.

When I practise mindfulness, I learn to observe my thoughts, body, emotions, senses and spirit. This awareness will create an understanding of my personal stories and experiences of my life, opening the door to my inner wisdom.

What would you like the story of your life to be?

Mindfulness Unlocked by Francis O' Toole

45. Enlightenment

"Kindness is more important than wisdom, and the recognition of that is the beginning of wisdom."
— Theodore Rubin

People within a small community went to the Oracle Rhema to see whether it was possible to achieve enlightenment. They told the Oracle Rhema they were trying to change things they dislike about themselves but found this was a struggle because they were merely pushing it underground or becoming angry with themselves. The Oracle Rhema said, *"Suppressing feelings and emotions is leading you into depression."*

Looking into their eyes, the Oracle Rhema could see they were continuing to search for answers to their questions.

The Oracle Rhema continued, *"Enlightenment will occur unexpectedly when we love ourselves and love others as they are, when we accept the things we cannot change, change the things we can and ask the universe for wisdom to know the difference."*

Mindfulness invites me to open the door of my heart, embracing and accepting things as they are. It is okay to ask questions but accept if there are times I cannot come up with an answer. I need to be patient with every unresolved issue of my heart. When I can live with the questions, perhaps in time without even knowing it, I will find my way to the answers, thus achieving enlightenment.

Allow yourself time to consider in a non judgemental way:

1. Are there feelings or emotions that you are suppressing?

2. Are there areas of your life that you need to accept rather than to try to change?

46. Careers

"Simplicity is the ultimate sophistication." —
Leonardo da Vinci

A young man came to the Oracle Rhema to discuss and look for advice on the career pathways he should be considering. The Oracle Rhema asked, *"What is your academic and work experience to date?"* The Oracle Rhema listened for a long time to the reply of the young man. On hearing all of it, the Oracle Rhema was in no doubt but the young man had many skills, talents and abilities.

Yet, the young man was unhappy and confused about what he wanted to do with his life. When he shared his fears and self doubt, the Oracle Rhema invited the young man to a local swimming pool.

She asked the young man to do the following, *"Jump into the pool and remain underwater for more than forty five seconds."* When the time was up, the young man came up gasping for oxygen. The Oracle Rhema then turned to the young man and said, *"You know you have chosen the right career when you want it as badly as the need to breathe."*

Mindfulness awareness when choosing a career pathway is really important. There are many unhappy people in careers, who just don't want to be there. If our career is based on self-reflection, we choose a career that matches our values and is aligned with our inner being — then we have chosen our career mindfully. If we are in a career where we are unhappy or unfulfilled, maybe it's time to find our inner strength and consider a career change. There are wonderful opportunities for people to return to college as mature students.

When we have mindfully reflected on what we want out of our careers, this will help us choose the right career; for example, if you want to share your talents and ability with young people, then teaching could be the career for you.

Your CV and job interview require a lot of preparation. Take time to reflect and talk with others who have experience and knowledge in these areas. We all need to take ownership of our careers and put in place an action plan that will focus on the positive. Seek out career experts who are willing to give their advice on how best to decide on your career choice, it will be a good investment towards your future. Employers are looking for the following key skills: critical and creative thinking skills, ability to collaborate and communicate, flexibility, initiative, productivity and leadership. From a very young age, family members and neighbours asked, *"What career will you choose?"* I knew that I always wanted to work with people. In the course of my life, I worked in the following professions: hotel and catering, active ministry, chaplain, teacher, guidance counsellor, career coach and psychotherapist. The average young person leaving school today will make eight career changes during their working life.

The most important thing when choosing a career mindfully is that it is right for you. Believe in yourself, dream of great things and know with hard work you will achieve it. It is so important to be mindfully aware with every breath to trust in the process, stay present and real, treat yourself with loving kindness.

Mindfulness Unlocked by Francis O' Toole

1. How well does your current career match your values?

2. Is your career allowing you to share your talents and abilities?

3. Is it time to change career direction?

Mindfulness Unlocked by Francis O' Toole

47. Awareness In Work

"You can only lose what you cling to." — Buddha

A young employee became very stressed with his workload and went to the Oracle Rhema seeking advice. The Oracle Rhema said, *"If you just sit and observe, you will see how restless your mind can be"*. After a brief moment, the Oracle continued, *"When we calm our mind to be in the present moment, our intuition will start to blossom; it will boost our energy levels, making us feel good"*.

I find the working environment challenging, stimulating and demanding. There are times when I am meant to be many things to different people. My day could involve meetings, answering the phone, dealing with one to one conversations, conflict resolution, use of ICT, group work, presentations, etc. I have caught my mind becoming overactive and full of demands. The danger is getting too stressed — for me this is how I experience it: tightness in my chest, shortness in my breath, muscle pain, inability to concentrate; my body is carrying the stress to enable my mind continue with the work.

When stress creeps in, I observe what is going on in my body at that moment — I decide to take a few minutes to myself. I consciously become aware of my breath, inhaling and exhaling — sensing the rise and fall of my chest. I stay with this for one minute before heading back into the routine of work. If this is not working, I go for a short walk around the building, walking tall and becoming aware of my breath. I find both of these short exercises renew my body and mind leaving me refreshed to continue with my work.

1. To mindfully monitor your stress level, ask yourself on a scale of 1 to 10 where is your current work related stress level? 1 = very little stress, 10 = very high stress.

2. What are the triggers of work-related stress for you?

3. What strategies do you have for managing work-related stress?

Mindfulness Unlocked by Francis O' Toole

48. The Working Environment

"If you want to conquer the anxiety of life, live in the moment, live in the breath." — Amit Ray

In Ireland, National Workplace Wellbeing Day is celebrated and takes place annually with hundreds of businesses getting involved. Fortunately more and more employers across Ireland are interested in the wellbeing of their employees. More than 500 businesses were involved in 2017. It is great to see companies of all types and sizes taking the initiative and getting involved with this project. There are many benefits for companies who actively participate in the wellbeing day. For example, it helped to foster healthy professional relationships, increased the level of happiness among employees and there was a notable reduction in absenteeism. The slogan was: *"Have fun while caring for our wellbeing."*

The Irish Government has now put Wellbeing on the curriculum for all Junior Cycle students and has a National Policy Priority Programmes managed by the HSE. The business world and the world of academics are recognising the huge importance of wellbeing and mindfulness. Lucky for me, I have the privilege of teaching mindfulness to teenagers and to large companies.

I invite you to reflect on the following questions to help focus on wellbeing:

1. Who can you turn to for encouragement, reassurance and support when in doubt?

2. Do you have a safe place where you can be yourself? Will this be with a partner, friend, sibling or parent?

3. Name some healthy distractions or 'me time' such as exercise, yoga, music, cooking, reading.

4. Are there unhealthy or unhelpful habits that you need to change?

I find the following strategies very helpful when I want to unwind:

- ❏ Meditation.

- ❏ Get more sleep: 7–8 hours a night.

- ❏ Drink less caffeine and alcohol.

- ❏ Cut down on the amount of time given to TV/ social media.

- ❏ Doing something creative e.g. practise cooking, singing, dancing, art, music.

- ❏ Have a non-work-related chat with a colleague.

- ❏ Prepare a healthy meal.

- ❏ Let loose and have a good laugh.

- ❏ Give a genuine compliment.

- ❏ Do a random act of kindness.

- ❏ Spend time with loved ones.

Mindful awareness of my actions in the present moment allows my mind to relax and increase my state of wellbeing. This state of wellbeing allows for greater enjoyment of health, happiness and contentment.

49. Mindfulness At Work

"Perfection of character is this: to live each day as if it were your last, without frenzy, without apathy, without pretence." — Marcus Aurelius

I have found that many of the work activities I do daily are repeated practises. The danger is taking things for granted. To give an example; I go to my office every morning, take out my key and unlock the door. I do it automatically without thinking. Now I am developing my skill of awareness, I stop and pause before unlocking the door. I take a deep breath and compose myself before embarking on a long day of activities. This exercise reminds me of having mindful awareness in all my work activities.

Now I have an awareness of the danger of doing things on automatic pilot and maybe not giving the proper attention required. Hence, I take occasional moments to stop and cultivate purposeful awareness of what activity I am about to do. The result: no sleepwalking and I interact with all activities 100%.

I invite you to reflect on the following questions to develop mindfulness at work:

1. Do you feel that you work on autopilot?

2. How well do you present yourself to work each day?

3. Do you stop, take a deep breath and reflect before you present yourself to all daily activities?

Mindfulness Unlocked by Francis O' Toole

50. Mindfulness Sitting At Work

"Stay present for the 'now' of your life. It's your point of power." — Doug Dillon

Our working environment can be challenging and stressful. Mindfulness sitting at work allows me to unwind and to be present in the 'now' moment.

I invite you to consider mindful sitting as part of your daily routine, especially as a way to unwind from stressful situations or events. The questions will help you focus:

1. How do you sit? Is your body posture open or closed?

2. Do you spend a lot of time sitting at a desk?

3. Do you feel tension in your muscles, for example, across your shoulders?

How to sit mindfully:

1. Take off your shoes and place your feet firmly on the floor.

2. Become aware of your posture — sit comfortably with your back straight.

3. Pay attention to your breath and notice the natural rhythm of the breath.

4. In the next breath, inhale counting 1-2-3-4-5 then exhale counting from 1 to 7.

5. Observe your thoughts and notice your feelings.

6. Consider a word or phrase of inspiration for this day before returning to your work.

7. Then when you are ready to open your eyes, continue with the normal routine of the day.

51. Stress

"The body and mind are intrinsically linked. Stress and anxiety are the root of many illnesses, we need to listen to our minds to prevent them." — Jayne Morris

When experiencing stress and high anxiety, I could be compared to the ship at sea caught up in a mighty storm. When in this situation there is absolutely no escape: I have to ride the storm until it passes or wait for docking in the next harbour. I need to be aware that when I am stressed out or experiencing high anxiety, hormones like cortisol flood my body, producing a fight or flight response. My heart rate goes up, I experience sweating, even quicker breath intake and find it difficult to concentrate or focus.

The physical sensations I experience when stressed or suffering from high anxiety are uncomfortable but they're still only physical sensations. My body will want to run or take flight to avoid this physical sensation. This is often called fight or flight response. Mindfulness is inviting me to become aware of and embrace my physical sensations, accepting them as they are. Stress is the body's normal response to a challenge, threat or excitement. Coping with stress can lead to resilience and a sense of achievement. I am aware that I have had different levels of stress in my life. I experience stress when the stress level is high enough to motivate me into action and accomplishing things e.g. I always experience stress before exams. I have often found myself full of distress when I got really bad news or I felt unsure of what to do next e.g. when I heard of the death of a friend. I am aware of some who come to me for counselling and they suffer from chronic stress which can lead to low self-esteem, depression, suicidal thinking, anxiety disorders, poor physical health. When I meet people with chronic stress, I tend to reach out to see if I can lead them in developing coping strategies, which will assist with future management of adversity.

Stress is calling me to be like the sails of a mighty ship, bending with the wind.

It's important when I feel stress to find something that will help me to distract from that stress and to focus on a new way of thinking. There are times when I have to admit I am under pressure and seek new ways of dealing with it. This can be difficult and challenging but adapting to new ways will allow me to journey in a new direction. Stress can be fearful but it can also be used to motivate me in a new direction. For example, I could use my senses to help me when I feel uncomfortable or overwhelmed in any way whatsoever.

The following mindfulness exercise focusing on the senses has helped me to become grounded. This means I will be present to my body and connected to the world around me. This experience allows me to feel centred and balanced no matter what's going on around me. I invite you to try the following exercise:

1. With the gift of sight, think of five things that you can see right now.

2. With the gift of hearing, think of four things you can hear right now.

3. With the gift of touch, think of three things that you can touch right now.

4. With the gift of smell, name two things that you can smell right now.

5. With the power of your breath, take one very deep breath inhaling goodness and continue with the exhale of negative feelings and emotions.

This very simple exercise focusing on the senses is often used in mindfulness to help keep us in the present moment and to help reduce stress and anxiety.

I know that creating awareness of stress will enable me to deal with it. I have learned to allow my mind to stay focused. I keep telling myself that the storm will pass, embracing the challenge. The experience after every storm will be one of guaranteed peace. I give myself positive messages: *"Don't jump ship, learn to bend with the challenges of life."* Every now and then I take time to pause: with my two feet on the ground, I focus on the in breath and out breath, thus reducing stress.

52. Resilience

"Waste not fresh tears over old grief." — Euripides

The Oracle Rhema told a story about a young boy who had been advised at an early stage to leave school because he had poor academic ability. The boy had got himself a job in the local hotel as a waiter. After a few years there was a change of management. When the new manager heard the young boy was unable to read or write, he sacked him.

Now a young man, he got a job as a car salesperson and proved his ability with such a high performance that he was able to purchase his own garage after a few years. He subsequently became very wealthy.

A journalist heard of the great achievement of this man and contacted him to do an article for the local newspaper. On hearing the man's story, the journalist said, *"Imagine what you could achieve if you were able to read and write."* to which the man responded, *"I would still be a waiter."*

Mindfulness empowers me to embrace my gifts, talents and abilities. I always strive to dream of great things, believing they are possible to achieve. I find the words of Robert Goddard inspirational: *"It is difficult to say what is impossible, for the dream of yesterday is the hope of today and the reality of tomorrow."*

Mindfulness Unlocked by Francis O' Toole

53. Mindfulness For Sleeping At Night

"Too many of us are not living our dreams because we are living our fears." — Les Brown

There is no better medicine for all of us to recover from a busy day than a good night's sleep. I find it really important to relax before going to bed, for me this means switching off the mobile phone, social media and the TV twenty minutes before going to bed.

While exercise is really good for us, I try to avoid a lot of exercise at night time because it stimulates the brain and warms up the body. This will not help if I want to be in a sleepy mood.

In the morning when I get out of bed, I spend care and time making my bed for the night ahead knowing I will return when ready for a good night's sleep.

I certainly enjoy my morning coffee but I try to avoid caffeine after 4pm as it interferes with my sleep.

Watching what I eat before going to bed is also crucial. While it's important to ensure I eat the right foods during the day with veg and fruit — I try not to eat a few hours before bedtime. I have found eating late at night before going to bed can give me heartburn and indigestion resulting in a poor night's sleep.

I try to have regular sleep patterns, going to bed at the same time at night and getting up at the same time in the morning. This helps the body clock to know when it's bedtime. I also have an alarm on my phone to remind me it's near bedtime thirty minutes before I head to bed.

I always get my clothes ready for the next day. This helps me to relax and prevents me wondering during the night whether I am prepared for the next day. In preparation for the next day, I bring any work issues, emails, social media, etc. to a close at a reasonable time. I like to keep a to-do list that can wait for the next day. This allows me the freedom to stop worrying about work-related issues.

Alcohol disrupts my sleep, so I try to avoid a night cap, especially if I have work the next day.

When in bed, I place myself in a mindful presence by reflecting on the day. I close my eyes, become aware of my breath and observe how I feel. I focus on my mood, my emotions or what I am thinking. I look back over the day, noticing times when I was mindful and maybe not so mindful.

I identify three things I was happy with during the day. I bring this positive image to mind.

This allows me to give thanks and gratitude for the good things in my life.

54. Disrupted Sleep

"To meditate is to listen with a receptive heart."
— Shakyamuni Buddha

There are many people who attend counselling because they experience high anxiety and lots of stress resulting in poor sleep at night. When they wake, thoughts enter their minds about their daily activities or upcoming events as they twist and turn in bed. They have shared with me that they get up during the night to have something to eat or go onto social media as a distraction. Their night's sleep is broken, resulting in the person feeling grumpy the next day.

Setting the scene for a good night's sleep is crucial. I always make sure the room is as dark as possible with curtains pulled tightly, the windows slightly open for fresh air and the mobile phone in flight mode, ensuring no disturbances. I am told by an ICT consultant that the blue light from your phone and iPad interferes with the sleep-inducing hormone melatonin. It would be best to have the phone out of your room at night.

I practise the following if I awake during the night and encourage you to do likewise:

Instead of getting out of bed, I become aware of my surroundings. I tell myself that I am safe and comfortable. Then I become aware of my breath, taking deep breaths. I become aware of the rising and falling of my chest as I inhale and exhale. I may practise this for five or ten minutes, until I find my mind resting, leaving me in a comfortable state and this allows for sleep.

As part of my journal work, I keep a record of my sleep pattern and note what may have disturbed my sleep, which could be a late coffee, worrying about work issues or anxiety. When I track my sleep patterns and note what's having a negative impact, my awareness allows me to put a positive sleeping plan in place.

Looking through my journal I know that taking deep breaths allows my whole body to relax. This definitely works when trying to sleep. I also do the following: once my body is feeling comfortable, I close my eyes and picture myself lying in a boat out in the middle of a very calm ocean looking up at an incredible blue sky full of stars. I stay with this image until sleep sets in. This I do most nights, tricking my brain into the belief that it's time to rest and sleep. A good night's sleep will refresh my body, mind and emotional wellbeing. It's widely accepted that we all need seven to eight hours sleep at night in order to restore our energy levels to embrace our daily challenges.

Sleep

Sleep,
Deep in resting,
Doors shut,
Darkness sets in,
The world no more.

Safety is felt,
Warm and glowing,
Comfort of the womb.

Mindfulness Unlocked by Francis O' Toole

The ship afloat,
Rocks on the sea,
Waves beat like a drum.

Heartbeat rhythm
Flows with life
Eternal.

55. Religion

"We can bring our spiritual practice into the streets, into our communities when we see each realm as a temple, as a place to discover that which is sacred."
— Jack Kornfield

The Oracle Rhema was always able to be true to herself; others began to think she was a rebel.

Yet, they all had a common belief that the Oracle Rhema had special qualities about her, with a beautiful smile and warm welcome, never offending anyone. She seemed to have a good connection with nature and with people, even those who had a different belief system than her.

The people gathered around the Oracle Rhema to seek answers to the many questions they had about life. They wanted to know if religion was the answer to the world's problems and, if so, what religion should they follow?

The Oracle Rhema responded, *"If in doubt, create your own religion."* I follow the Christian gospels based on love and it reassures us of God's presence in our daily life: *"Where two or three are gathered in my name, I am with them."* (Matthew 18:20)

Mindfulness invites me to, *"Teach what I believe and to believe what I teach"* but never follow others with *'blind obedience'*. When I am true to myself, I am completely honest and real. It is my duty to follow my informed conscience: *"The truth will set you free."* (John 8:32)

I want to get through life knowing I did the right thing by other people, treating all people with respect and kindness.

I believe religion is an organised response by people to express their belief in the creator of the universe. Every religion will have different traditions, rituals and rites as an expression of their faith. For example, Hindus have a belief in multitudes of gods; Buddhists say there is no deity; new age spiritualists believe they are the god part of a higher power; Muslims believe in one God and Muhammad is a prophet; Christians believe in a loving God and Jesus is his son who came to Earth but was rejected by the people; Jews believe in the Old Testament in the Bible where God has chosen them as his people. All of these religions are helping people to respond to their God and live life to the best of their ability.

Mindfulness has helped me to be open to all world religions and to treat those who have a different religion from me with kindness and with no judgements. Over the course of my life, I have attended ceremonies in different religions: Orthodox church, Hindus and Buddhist temples, Jewish synagogues. I even got the opportunity to visit the Sheikh Zayed Grand Mosque in Abu Dhabi, the capital city of the United Arab Emirates. It's the largest mosque in the country. I was comfortable to sit here for twenty minutes of silent meditation. I found peace, hospitality and respect in each of these places of worship. I believe both mindfulness and religion can complement each other as they are guiding our lives to have depth and meaning.

When in the Middle East, I went up to the top of the Burj Khalifa, a skyscraper in Dubai — with a total height of 829.8 metres, it is the tallest building in the world. It is a very impressive sight to see the wealth of the country displayed in this mighty building and city. Yet, mindful awareness reminds me that real wealth and real religion

Mindfulness Unlocked by Francis O' Toole

are best understood when we reach out to the poor and those alienated in society. This is best summed up by quoting Sheikh Zayed bin Sultan Al Nahyan, late President and founder of the United Arab Emirates, *"Real wealth is the hard work that benefits both a person and the community. It is immortal and eternal, and becomes the value of the person and the nation."*

Mindfulness Unlocked by Francis O' Toole

56. Theology

"The true aim of everyone who aspires to be a teacher should be, not to impart his own opinions, but to kindle minds." — Frederick W. Robertson

A well-known Theologian came to seek advice from the Oracle Rhema. He told the Oracle Rhema that he had spent all of his life reading the scriptures, in prayer and even in moments in solitude. He went on to share that his feelings are of loneliness, isolation and he was very unhappy.

The Oracle Rhema complimented the Theologian for his dedication and commitment to his beliefs.

She then asked the Theologian, *"What is your goal in life?"* The Theologian responded, *"My goal is to follow the teachings of the Bible and then I will be rewarded with eternal life."*

The Oracle Rhema then said, *"My friend, why not embrace this life: live, laugh, experience fun and love? When you achieve this, you will be ready for the next life."*

The cornerstone of Buddha's philosophy is based on the belief that changing one's thoughts can change one's reality. This is a fundamental principle which is the driving force behind the modern day effective counselling technique cognitive behaviour therapy (CBT). My own motto is *"Change the way you think, change your life."* Many ancient philosophers claimed that happiness was achieved and controlled by our thoughts; for example, the philosopher Epictetus (50–135 AD), influenced by Socrates, puts it: *"What concerns me is not the way things are, but rather the way people think things are."*

I am not surprised that there is an increase in the number of people who have taken an interest recently in the area of mindfulness, especially with the decline in the numbers of people following organised religions. People like to have security and a belief system as part of their lives.

Mindfulness is not aimed at replacing people's religious beliefs or faith practices, rather it is there to enhance and embrace people's lives. Mindfulness is offering all people a new way of thinking: *"creating mindful awareness to the present moment."* More and more studies and scientific research are proving that living in the present moment mindfully is certainly helping people to think differently, improving their cognitive ability and adding to their wellbeing.

I am a person of Christian faith rooted in Celtic spirituality, who has embarked on the journey of using the philosophy of mindfulness in my daily life. Since I embraced mindfulness, I have experienced a reduction in stress and anxiety. It would be a fallacy to conclude that mindfulness happens automatically because I completed a course. I need to work on the skills of mindfulness daily, constantly creating awareness of where I am at in the present moment until it becomes a way of life and part of who I am as a person.

Mindfulness needs commitment, practice and time for it to work in my life. Every time I consciously become aware of my breath, it allows me to renew my commitment to living mindfulness awareness. Every breath reminds me that each passing moment brings a new opportunity to choose for myself new beginnings.

Mindfulness Unlocked by Francis O' Toole

57. Living Life

"If you want to change the world, start with the next person who comes to you in need."
— B. D. Schiers

People gathered to listen to the Oracle Rhema talk about how best to live life. They had often heard her talk about the importance of mindfulness. A Rabbi was present in the group and wondered where could he do a short course on mindfulness. He would then have a qualification and certificate to place on his office wall along with all his Diplomas of achievement. The Oracle Rhema responded to the man, *"There is no comparable eloquence for mindfulness."* She went on to explain, *"When we have conscious awareness of the present moment in a kind, gentle and non-judgemental manner, we are living mindfulness. This conscious awareness is not a destination to reach or qualification to be achieved but seeing awareness as a companion on the journey of life."*

Mindfulness is a way of living, having constant awareness in the present moment. This happens each time I connect and observe my breath, appreciating the gift of life every day, every moment, 86,400 seconds daily. The truth of living is found in doing ordinary things in life in a mindful way. Then when I have achieved this, I continue to do the ordinary in an extraordinary way.

Mindfulness Unlocked by Francis O' Toole

58. Eternal Life

"Always hold fast to the present. Every situation, indeed every moment, is of infinite value, for it is the representative of a whole eternity."
— Johann Wolfgang von Goethe

A group of theologians and philosophers gathered to discuss the existence of eternal life. They wondered whether such places called heaven and hell existed. They called on the Oracle Rhema to hear whether she had any advice about what an afterlife would look like.

The Oracle Rhema responded by telling a story: *"Many people are gathered at a banquet, sitting at a table with plenty of food and wine. There was one difference among the people at the banquet: the people sitting around the table were thin and sickly. They appeared to be famished. They were holding spoons with very long handles and each found it possible to reach into the pot of stew and take a spoonful, but because the handle was longer than their arms, they could not get the spoons back into their mouths.*

A man shuddered at the sight of their misery and suffering. God said, "You have seen Hell."

Behind the second door, the room appeared exactly the same. There was a large round table with the large pot of wonderful stew that made the man's mouth water. The people had the same long-handled spoons, but they were well nourished and plump, laughing and talking.

The man said, "I don't understand."

God smiled. "It is simple," he said, "Love only requires one skill. These people learned early on to share and feed one another. While the greedy only think of themselves."

The good people were not hungry because they could pick up the food and place it in the mouths of others. Whereas those experiencing hell were hungry; they could pick up the food but were too greedy and refused to place it in the mouths of others."

Paradise is created in the world when we strive to care for others with love, kindness and generosity."

The Oracle Rhema left them guessing: was she talking about the eternal life or this life?

Mindfulness awareness is challenging me to focus on the present moment in caring and sharing. When I reach out to care for others, I stop being self-centred and I get the opportunity to practise loving kindness. I have the ability to create paradise in this world every time I am willing to share, care and be fair.

Mindfulness Unlocked by Francis O' Toole

59. Flourishing

"In today's rush, we all think too much, seek too much, want too much and forget about the joy of being."
— Eckhart Tolle

The Oracle Rhema was overheard one day saying, *"All people have a mission."* When asked by some of those gathered to give more detail, she responded, *"To grow and flourish."* One of his followers decided to go out and preach this mission to people locally and internationally.

He first met with the Oracle Rhema, looking for her blessing and seeking advice. He asked the Oracle Rhema, *"What preparation should I make for the journey?"* to which the Oracle Rhema replied, *"The first step is to discover your inner journey."* The Oracle Rhema pondered for a while before continuing with her advice, *"When you have achieved the ability to move from the mind to the heart, then you will know what to do when informing others."*

It was the philosopher Socrates who said, *"All people are born to flourish."* I believe this is a wonderful and beautiful concept about the purpose of life. We are all born equal with one mission: to find our *"heart's desire"* and to nurture it.

There is always the danger that I may neglect my innate ability and follow pathways that lead me astray. If I can mindfully continue to have gratitude for my gifts and talents, I know I will be able to *'flourish'* as a person.

There are so many ways to show gratitude, for example; just saying 'thanks' when others do kind deeds or do a good job at work. Giving a gift like a box of chocolates or a bunch of flowers is another way of saying thanks or bringing a friend out for a meal. I always get a nice warm feeling within when I generously give time, a gift or say kind words of thanks.

Mindfulness gratitude will enable me to respect and appreciate what others have done for me. It will also help me on my journey of self discovery, understanding my mission to '*grow and flourish*'.

Mindfulness Unlocked by Francis O' Toole

60. Simplicity

*"The colour of springtime is in the flowers; the
colour of winter is in the imagination."*
— Terri Guillemets

A Catholic Bishop invited his friend the Oracle Rhema for
lunch at the Bishop's palace. During a lengthy conversation
the Bishop sought her advice and wisdom on how to
achieve simplicity, to which the Oracle Rhema responded,
*"The first step to achieve simplicity is to let go of power
and control. The second step is to sell the palace and give
your wealth to the poor."*

The Bishop was not happy with this advice and put
forward all of the arguments possible to justify his
position on power and wealth. The Oracle Rhema then
asked, *"What would Jesus do?"*

Mindfulness is inviting me to see positions of authority as
a privileged opportunity to serve those whom I am
responsible for. There is always the danger that I can
become blind to the needs of those around me and go out
of my way to protect the institution.

Mindfulness invites me to ponder on the following
question: which is most important, to protect the
institution or to protect the people whom the institution is
meant to serve?

It would be easy to allow my life to focus on wealth,
richness and achievements but I believe having a
meaningful life is more important. I am reminded of an
experience I had while on holidays in Tunisia, a country in
the Maghreb region of North Africa. I got to visit an

amazing site, where the residents still live in underground houses. The earth and caves provide protection against the very hot summer heat and winter winds. Most of these homes are found around Matmata — this was Luke Skywalker's home in the 1977 Star Wars movie. The people I stayed with were very happy and seemed to be fulfilled. They lived very simple lives without technology, no luxury goods and a lot of their clothes were hand made. These people lived a life free from the stress of modern day living that we experience in the west. I asked one resident if she would like to move to a modern house. She replied, *"No, we could buy everything but not peace of mind."*

This experience reminded me that real wealth can be found in simplicity, leading us to happiness and peace of mind.

Mindfulness Unlocked by Francis O' Toole

61. Leaders

"Awareness is the greatest agent for change."
— Eckhart Tolle

The Oracle Rhema was asked the following question by a large gathering of people in the local community hall: *"Should leaders in the community have standards that match the value system of the community?"*

The Oracle Rhema responded by telling a story about two Hindu monks who were out walking when they came across this beautiful young woman who wanted to cross the river but was unable. The older monk offered to carry the woman through the water to the opposite side of the river. The monks then continued on their journey. After travelling for a while, the monks came to a resting place. Then the younger monk asked, *"Was it right to carry the woman across the river since we are celibate monks who've decided to have detachment from worldly pursuits, spending our life in contemplation of God?"* The older monk responded, *"I left the woman at the river but you rankle on continuing to carry her in your mind."*

The style of leadership I choose may have a different style or approach than others in leadership positions. I need to have awareness that my style is only authentic if I stop making judgements and criticising those who do things differently than me.

Mindful awareness allows me to understand the dangers of being self critical and judgemental towards others, running with a false storyline or fake news or gossip. I am constantly trying to create awareness of wasting my time and energy on small issues that may prevent me from seeing the bigger picture.

Mindfulness Unlocked by Francis O' Toole

62. Concept Of Mindfulness

"When you realise nothing is lacking, the whole world belongs to you." — Lao Tzu

A group of intellectuals gathered at an assembly to discuss and try to understand the concept of mindfulness. Gathered in this assembly were traditional theologians, artists and scientists. After much discussion and debate, the group failed to come up with a definition or meaning of mindfulness. They approached the Oracle Rhema to see what advice she would give.

The Oracle Rhema was only willing to share her understanding and meaning of mindfulness. The Oracle Rhema looked at each person individually and then addressed her answer to the gathered group by saying, *"Mindfulness is a personification of all those gathered here today."* Members who were gathered were looking confused and sought clarification.

The Oracle Rhema went on to explain, *"Mindfulness is allowing each person to reach their full potential, which is best done by embracing both science and ancient wisdom."*

The 'dictionary' definition of 'mindfulness' is *"a mental state achieved by one's awareness of the present moment, while calmly acknowledging and accepting one's feelings, thoughts and bodily sensations, used as a therapeutic technique."*

I like the idea of embracing science and ancient wisdom to define mindfulness. But what is really important are the skills I gain from using mindfulness. In the past I would walk in the park with a purpose of achieving a fitness level or trying to work out a problem on my mind. Mindfulness allows me to walk in the same park with comfort and ease, I am engaged in the moment. I now see the beauty of the sky with its many changing clouds. I hear the birds on the tall robust trees. I can touch and admire the beautiful colourful flowers. Day in and day out I am cultivating mindfulness, feeling a great sense of wellbeing while living with awareness in the present moment.

63. Art

"Nothing can harm you as much as your own thoughts unguarded." — Buddha

Whenever people gathered in the presence of the Oracle Rhema they were always commenting on how well she looked. She was always happy and at peace. One day a member of the community asked the Oracle Rhema, *"How can we be in control of our emotions and feelings?"* The Oracle Rhema replied, *"Speak slowly, have clear thoughts and be non-judgemental."*

She continued, *"When we are in control of our emotions, feelings and our way of thinking, this will allow for true awareness."*

I would always find time to visit an art gallery or museum when visiting a new city. This allows me time to reflect and to stop being a tourist. The Van Gogh Museum in Amsterdam allowed me the opportunity to stand back and reflect on the life of Van Gogh. I was really touched when learning about his mental health and how he struggled to cope with life. He struggled a great deal with mental health issues and even cut off his ear on 23 December 1888. This was probably the first public sign of his mental illness, but he had several mental breakdowns until his tragic death by suicide a year and a half later. This story really moved me and highlighted how fragile our mental health is.

I believe we all have a duty to be aware of our mental health and to work on having positive wellbeing. After my visit to the Van Gogh Museum, I took up artwork and this helps me to relax. It also allows my creativity and imagination to come alive. I find it relaxing picking the colours, mixing the paints and deciding what brush to use on the canvas. The great thing about doing artwork or even spending time admiring the artwork of another person is that it allows me to slow down and disengage temporarily from the busy world I experience all around me. When I stand back to admire art work I have to be very still, take in all the colours, look at the painting on canvas, ask myself about my interpretation of the painting, and analyse what message the artist is revealing to me.

Artwork facilitates me to be in touch with my thoughts and emotions. It allows me to be open to my creativity and imagination.

Mindfulness art enables me to cultivate an awareness of the world around me and the people I meet. Like art, mindfulness encourages me to be still and stand back, to take time admiring the beauty of the world and people around me. Mindfulness will be more than focusing on my emotions and feelings in relationships, it will become the brushstroke on the canvas of social interaction. This is best summed up in the words of Van Gogh, *"What would life be if we had no courage to attempt anything?"*

64. Stop And Look

"How many things I can do without!" — Socrates

The Sistine Chapel is in the Apostolic Palace, the official residence of the Pope in Vatican City, Rome. It is here between 1508 and 1512 Michelangelo spent all his time painting the Last Judgment above the altar. Pilgrims from all over the world from every religion and non religion come to visit this historical and beautiful building.

One day a visitor turned to the Oracle Rhema while admiring the beauty of the chapel and said, *"There is so much to see, I am rushing around but I can't take it all in."* to which the Oracle Rhema responded, *"Stop and look; take in one image at a time."*

To develop the *'stop and look'* skill of seeing one thing at a time, I decided to go to my garden and plant some seeds. I tended to them everyday, watering them when necessary, watching them grow and allowing the light to shine on the plants.

I call them my mindfulness plants, as I nurture and care for them. These plants will remind me that every time I *'stop and look'* at the plants, I am creating awareness of living in the present moment.

I found this *'stop and look'* mindfulness exercise helps me to have a sense of awe and wonder about nature and the world around me. It also helps me to be patient in the moment and to use my time wisely.

Feng Shui is a Chinese study that is more than a thousand years old. It considers how people interact with their environment and the subsequent energy that flows. This pseudoscience suggests having the right balance of objects and plants in our home or work environment to promote harmony.

I was given a Jade plant by a friend, which I placed in the front porch of my house. The Jade plant represents friendship. I am told the Jade plant is a magnet, a 'must have' in any household because it attracts money (I'm still waiting for this to happen!) I see the Jade plant as adding balance to my home, reminding me of the importance of hospitality. I know that caring for this Jade plant mindfully reminds me to see the importance of having balance of mind, body and spirit. Both the plants in my garden and the Jade plant are strong reminders of the importance to *'stop and look'*.

Mindfulness Unlocked by Francis O' Toole

65. Change

"Do every act of your life as though it were the very last act of your life." — Marcus Aurelius

After listening to the Oracle Rhema speak about the importance of living well, speaking the truth, being just and expressing kindness, one young man asked, *"How can we change bad habits we may have developed over time to replace them with good habits?"*

The Oracle Rhema responded, *"All humans respond to situations depending on our perception of events."*

She then said, *"If we can change our inner attitudes, we will have the ability to change our outer views on life."*

Mindfulness practice has helped me to observe my breath, my inner thoughts and emotions, giving me a new perspective on my experience.

My observer self has become reflective and open to gaining insight, generating change, leading to enlightenment.

I invite you to reflect on your thoughts, attitudes and behaviours — do you want to change any of these?

Mindfulness Unlocked by Francis O' Toole

66. Message

"The doors of wisdom are never shut."
— Benjamin Franklin

The Oracle Rhema was attending a commemoration ceremony where there was an unveiling of a statue to a great charismatic leader who had a vision for his people built on truth, justice and equality.

When asked for her opinion about the statue, the Oracle Rhema reflected and looked at the demeanour of the crowd before responding with the following statement: *"It is easier to build a shrine than to live the message."*

The practice of living mindfully can be extended to every aspect of my life, from sleeping to waking, from eating to exercising, from values to having a sense of spirituality. I can do everything mindfully once I am making every effort to do so. The most important thing is not to go on a journey where I am disingenuous with myself or others; I need to learn to be truthful with myself at all times.

Mindfulness Unlocked by Francis O' Toole

67. Rewards

"Walk as if you are kissing the earth with your feet."
— Thich Nhat Hanh

A preacher was rewarded by society for his wonderful contribution to the local community. He supported the building of a new church and the construction of a parish hall. He was an excellent fundraiser and was capable of getting projects completed.

In conversation with the Oracle Rhema, he was full of arrogance as he boasted about his achievements in life, but admitted failing to develop his faith. He asked the Oracle Rhema for advice on how he should develop his faith. The Oracle Rhema responded, *"The first step on the journey of inner belief is to realise that faith is a gift found in humility."*

Mindfulness allows me to have inner awareness of my values, faith and belief systems. If I am true to myself, I will connect more positively with the outer world around me. It is so important for me to express my gifts and talents with pride but not arrogance.

Mindfulness creates an inner belief where I can be real, authentic, humble and true to myself. This means I am not living by someone else's standards or rules. I am living as my natural self, which will have 'rewards' full of compassion and love.

68. New Eyes

"When we get caught up in the business of the world, we lose connection with one another and ourselves."
— Jack Kornfield

Gaudí's Sagrada Família Cathedral in Barcelona will have taken 144 years to construct by the time it's completed in 2026. The basilica, which was consecrated by Pope Benedict XVI in November 2010, attracts some three million tourists a year.

The Oracle Rhema was a regular visitor to the Cathedral and could be seen there at least once a year. She was asked by a tourist who was there for the first time, *"Why come back year after year?"* to which the Oracle Rhema responded, *"So I can see the progress with new eyes."*

Mindfulness invites me to see everything with new eyes, as it were my first time seeing. A good example of seeing with new eyes, is to watch the expression on a child's face when they see something for the first time; there is a genuine expression on their face of excitement-filled awe and wonder.

A cleric of Islam was asked if his faith gave meaning to his life to which he responded, *"Yes, I kept faithful to the five pillars of Islam: faith, prayer, charity, fasting and pilgrimage to Mecca. My pilgrimage to Mecca has given me a richer meaning to life, I now see all religion with 'new eyes' as people on a journey reaching their God in love and forgiveness.*

Mindfulness is not a religion but it invites those who practise religion to approach it with 'new eyes' to understand its values and beliefs. Both mindfulness and religion can complement each other as both invite us to live a life with an informed conscience living in harmony, peace and love.

69. Relationships

"All beings want to be happy, yet so very few know how. It is out of ignorance that any of us cause suffering, for ourselves or for others." — Sharon Salzberg

A group of religious leaders gathered at an assembly to discuss the importance of marriage as an institution. They argued for a long time and sought the opinions of some members of their community, who are among the 1.2 billion Roman Catholics worldwide. After much debate and discussion they decided to maintain their long traditional belief which served them well for many years. They defined marriage as a *"contract between a man and woman for the purpose of procreation."* This, they said, is written in the Code of Canon Law, which is the fundamental law for the Roman Catholic Church.

Some members of the community were left in doubt about what the hierarchy had to say since they were not qualified in the area of Theology. They felt this was a poignant moment and went to the Oracle Rhema seeking her advice about the contract of marriage. The Oracle Rhema requested the Bible for viewing; after careful reflection she quoted the New Testament 1 John 4:16 *"God is love and where there is love, there is God."*

The people of Ireland recognised the importance of all types of relationships. I am proud that we became the first country to legalise same-sex marriage by popular vote. The Irish thirty-fourth Amendment of the Constitution (Marriage Equality Act 2015) was amended, permitting marriage to be contracted by two people of the same sex.

Mindfulness has helped me to move beyond my traditional thinking of marriage between man and woman. Through mindfulness, I develop my awareness and ability to be open to and accepting of different types of relationships. The most important value for me is to be non-judgemental. We are all free to follow laws and rules of our religion, but be mindful that laws can create barriers to love. In all relationships, mindfulness is inviting me to observe my interactions with others, respect people's decisions and always be open to forgive.

All marriages in Ireland have a required legal element, which all couples must abide by. I founded Celtic Spirituality in 2017. Celtic Spirituality is about respecting, loving and caring for each other, the environment and all of nature. The Creator of the Universe has given us a beautiful gift of nature that is essential to our wellbeing. In January 2018, I registered as a Celtic Spirituality celebrant for weddings on the Register of Solemnisers. Celtic Spirituality weddings embrace all cultures and beliefs: it allows for interfaith weddings, Christian weddings or for those with no faith traditions.

70. Listening

"The stiller you are the calmer life is."
— Rasheed Ogunlaru

The Oracle Rhema always told stories and gave her advice to those who were willing to listen. One day a visitor to the community asked the Oracle Rhema, *"Do people always listen to your words of wisdom?"*

To which the Oracle Rhema responded, *"They listen but do they hear? Poverty still exists, there are many people living in homeless accommodation, the prisons are full, injustice continues, doctors are afraid of miracles and priests are unable to believe their message."*

I spend time in my beautiful garden daily listening to the sound of the birds and watching plants blowing in the wind.

When I listen attentively to the sound of nature, it allows me to develop a deeper level of alertness to be open to the sound of the human voice.

Mindfulness helps me to be vigilant when I am listening to others speak — be it family, friends, work colleagues or attending a class. It helps me to pay attention to the words of others as they speak, knowing that it is so easy to be distracted by many other things that may be going on at the same time.

When I listen mindfully, I hear exactly what the other person is saying. It allows my emotions and feelings to connect with empathy to the speaker. The message of the speaker may move me into taking some kind of spontaneous action if I am inspired by their words.

Research shows that only ten percent of us really listen effectively. Many of us are so distracted by modern day pressure, stress, and social media — not to mention the everyday to-do list that must be completed. We may think we are listening but our minds are jumping constantly thinking of what to say next or thinking about all of the other distractions going on in our heads.

I use the following questions as a guide to help me to listen mindfully:

Am I fully present to the speaker?

Am I listening in a non-judgemental way that allows me to hear the real message?

Am I motivated and inspired by the speaker?

Listening mindfully cultivates awareness of my needs and the needs of others. It allows my mind to be receptive to new ideas, leading me to creativity. It opens my heart to have passion and love. This is best described by Raji Lukkoor, *"Respond, don't react. Listen, don't talk. Think, don't answer."*

71. Equality

"For peace of mind, we need to resign as general manager of the universe." — Larry Eisenberg

The Oracle Rhema was invited to speak about equality at a major ecclesiastical conference. Gathered at this conference were leaders within the Catholic Church and other leaders of religious congregations. Before the Oracle Rhema spoke, she was instructed by a young priest on how best to address the prominent people gathered:

> A Cardinal — Your Eminence
>
> An Archbishop — Your Grace
>
> An ordinary Bishop — My Lord
>
> A vicar general — Monsignore
>
> A parish priest — Very Reverend Father
>
> A regular priest — Reverend Father
>
> Head of a monastery — Abbot
>
> Head of a female religious order — Very Reverend Mother

The Oracle Rhema began her speech, *"Greetings brothers and sisters in Christ. Equality is created when we do not have privileges because of a title and when we have a culture of respect where all people are of equal status."*

Mindfulness enables us to embrace others as we reach out in respect, kindness and equality.

I invite you to observe daily how well you communicate with the people you meet. Are you authentic, respectful, treating all equally?

72. Community

"Our task must be to free ourselves by widening our circle of compassion to embrace all living creatures and the whole of nature and its beauty." — Albert Einstein

The dignitaries, leaders and members of a small community wanted to establish norms and best practice for the people to follow, ensuring harmony, peace and love. They gathered all the people into their local hall to explore and brainstorm the following question:

"How best should we live our life?"

After failing to come to any definite conclusions, they put the same question to the Oracle Rhema. She took her time in responding and eventually made the following statement: *"Live in the moment, trusting in your inner belief."* After a pause, she continued: *"Each of us is born with closed fists; try to live life with open hands."*

Most of us are lucky to be born into family life where we will be supported and loved as we grow up by our parents, family, teachers and the people in our community. This feeling that we are supported and loved by others will give us peace of mind and a good sense of wellbeing. Mindful awareness invites me to acknowledge all those who play an important part in my daily life. It also invites me to consider reaching out as a leader and be supportive in my community as I get older. We all can play our part in being a positive role model to younger people, building a caring community and having a healthy environment.

There are many different ways in which I can be a leader in the community: for example, doing voluntary work, keeping the environment clean and tidy, donating time and money to the homeless, visiting the sick in hospital or old people living alone, supporting organisations like the St. Vincent de Paul Society or helping with the local youth clubs.

I have experienced many positive benefits since becoming a leader in my community, for example, making new friends, feeling positive about myself, gaining a sense of achievement, getting to know more about the community and the people who depend on it. This connection with the community enables me to grow maturely, have a feel-good factor and increase my wellbeing.

I invite you to reflect on the following questions:

1. Name something within the community that you are grateful for.

2. List the things you are proud of, especially when caring for others.

3. How have you reached out to family, friends and the people within your community?

I am always inspired when I see people like Prince Harry and Meghan Markle give of their time and energy to people in need. The British honours system awards medals and decorations to people for acts of bravery and to those who give a major contribution in the service of their community. I salute the incredible people in Ireland who are recipients of the annual Rehab People of the Year Awards for their contribution to the community.

On a recent visit to Washington DC, I had the privilege of visiting the 4-H Youth Development program, which is the largest youth development programme in the world. I noticed the following statement printed in bold letters on the wall of their canteen: *"Young people who volunteer their time to do good deeds, just two hours a week, are 50% less likely to smoke, drink alcohol or do drugs"*. Head, heart, hands and health are the four H's and they are the values members work on through fun and engaging programs.

Mindfulness enables me to create awareness of the wonderful people in our community and to be inspired by their actions of service. Mindfulness is inviting us to follow the example of people who give of their time generously but most of all mindfulness is inviting us to do the ordinary acts of service in an extraordinary way.

Mindfulness Unlocked by Francis O' Toole

73. Ring On Finger

"Great leaders have three things: inner light, inner vision and inner strength." — Amit Ray

Before the advancement of science and the understanding of the body, the Ancient Greeks believed that a vein ran directly from the third finger on the left hand to the heart. In Latin this is called the 'vena amoris' — vein of love. It is also said that the Egyptians worshipped the Sun and Moon and a ring was a symbol of the spirits. The ring has no beginning and no end. The Christians call this Alpha and Omega when talking about their God. In many European countries, we wear a ring on this finger to publicly express that we are married or engaged, showing our undying love for the other person.

Those who wear a ring on the third finger of the right hand traditionally represented power or service, for example, Bishops, Kings, Princes, etc. Pope Francis wears a ring on the third finger of his right hand as a sign of service to the gospel of Christ and his responsibility as leader of the Catholic Church.

People will wear rings for many reasons, traditions, beliefs or just for the sake of wearing jewellery.

The Oracle Rhema was asked about her understanding of wearing rings to which she replied, *"Several times a day I place my thumb on my left hand on the third finger to remind me I love myself and others love me."* She then went on to say, *"Several times a day I place my thumb on my right hand on the third finger to remind me, "I am amazing and capable of doing great things."*

I wear a ring on the third finger of my right hand. For me, it represents the presence of God in my daily life, guiding and directing me.

Whether you wear a ring or not, I invite you to reflect on the gift of love and commitment. I also invite you to reflect on the goodness of others who give of their time and service for the good of the community.

Mindfulness is inviting me to believe and trust in my inner light, inner vision and inner strength.

74. Love Is A Gift

"The personal life deeply lived always expands into truths beyond itself." — Anais Nin

A young celibate priest fell in love with one of his parishioners. One day he decided to send her a text to let her know that he was madly in love with her. He described his emotions and feelings and how he was fixated on her beauty. He concluded that he wanted to spend his time with her.

The following Sunday the woman attended the celebration of the Eucharist in the Cathedral along with 500 parishioners. Midway through the service the woman stood up and said, *"If you love me so much, come now and hug me."*

The Oracle Rhema asks the following question of us, *"How do you think this story ended?"*

Mindfulness is inviting me not to be shallow in relationships but to have an awareness of the quality of my relationships. If a relationship is to be meaningful, it needs to be real, authentic and honest. In relationships, I need to be aware of how my perceptions can influence my behaviour. This is best described by Abraham Lincoln, *"We can complain because rose bushes leave thorns or rejoice because those bushes have roses".*

A real relationship is about spending time getting to know one another. It's about recognising that communication is the key to a strong relationship. The early conversations when a couple meets allows them to get to know one another on a deeper level. I believe a relationship will be strengthened when a couple has the freedom to share what is going on in their lives, be it about family, friendships and all of life's wonders and wounds. When we can do this, we are talking about how life shaped us and contributed to who we are today. This level of communication will allow us to find real love. It will allow us to see love as a gift that maybe came unexpectedly but has the potential to grow even deeper. When the other person is there supporting you through both the good times and challenging times, this will be the real proof of love in action.

A relationship could be compared to that of a kite and an anchor. Sometimes one person soars and needs an anchor and sometimes the other person wants to soar and be supported. Real love in action is the promise to each other about being attuned to one another's feelings and goals, and giving one another what is most needed, when it's needed.

Many people want to make a public expression of their love and get married.

As a registered solemniser, it's a wonderful privilege to support couples planning and then performing the wedding ceremony mindfully. It's really special to see all of the ideas that couples come up with for their wedding, from sharing stories, reading poems, exchanging gifts, jumping the broom: there are so many rites and rituals. I enjoy working with couples to ensure their wedding day is special, unique and mindfully planned.

Marriage is their way of saying, *"I love you and I want to be with you."* Couples want to share their experiences and life together. They know by getting married, both want to share their life in a special commitment to each other.

Marriage is their way of saying, *"We are connected and want to be with each other"*, understanding there will be trials and tests as they plan their life together. I believe we all need to be mindful in our relationships, whether we are married or not. Relationships will demand awareness of intimacy, good communication and honesty if it is to grow and flourish.

Mindfulness Unlocked by Francis O' Toole

75. Breaking Down Boundaries

"Be kind whenever possible. It is always possible."
— Dalai Lama

A large group of politicians gathered in the local Government buildings to discuss ways of preventing migration. They expressed fears and concerns about those who came to their community from the Far East because they have different cultures, values, rituals, religion.

Lots of ideas and suggestions were floated about how this issue should be addressed, for example one idea was building a large border wall so that nobody could cross into the country without going through strict protocols: providing passports, visas, etc. The politicians then looked to the Oracle Rhema for moral support to justify their suggestions and arguments. The Oracle Rhema said one word: *"Respect."* She then went on to explain, *"Fears are built on a lack of knowledge and because of closed vision. If we show respect for others, they will respect us in return. I believe if we build walls or borders we are giving a clear message to others: 'you are not welcome here.'"*

Mindfulness strengthens my awareness to listening with respect, without judgements or arguments. This is best summed up by John F. Kennedy, *"For a city or a people to be truly free they must have the secure right, without economic, political or police pressure, to make their own choice and to live their own lives."* John F. Kennedy was reaching out to those who were alienated and marginalised in society.

As I was writing this chapter, I went to see the movie *Green Book*, based on a true story. Set in 1962, an Italian-

American, Tony Lip, is hired to be a chauffeur for African American pianist Dr. Don Shirley for a concert tour in the Deep South. The doctor is aware of the deep troubles he may encounter because of the colour of his skin and needs someone to act a driver and bodyguard. The green book was their guide to a few establishments that were safe for African Americans. They embarked on the journey and faced many difficult situations that ended up changing their lives forever. This movie brought to mind that real walls and boundaries are not just a physical identity supported with tight security, but the real walls are built in our mind: male and female stereotyping, discrimination against people because of their sex, race, age, religion, skin colour, members of an ethnic group, members of the travelling community.

Whenever we build physical walls or barriers, the end result is never good — just look at the Troubles in Northern Ireland to understand that barriers and walls do not work. The border in Northern Ireland led to constant violence, poverty, smuggling, a highly-expensive police force, and a lack of trust within the community. Whenever I go walking through Northern Ireland, I see evidence of this sad history. I also walked around the city of Dallas and came to the location where John F. Kennedy, the 35th President of the United States, was assassinated on November 22 1963 in Dallas, Texas. I also have to mention my visit to Ford's Theatre located in Washington D.C. It is famous for being the site of the assassination in April 1865 of Abraham Lincoln, the 16th President of the United States. Visiting each of these places reminds me of the importance of promoting peace and tolerance and having a strong opposition to all forms of violence and hatred.

Mindfulness Unlocked by Francis O' Toole

I am proud to be a citizen of the European Union; the EU endeavours to have no brick walls or boundaries between nations or individuals. We have a new European anthem, which comes from the Ninth Symphony composed in 1823 by Ludwig Van Beethoven when he set the music to *Ode to Joy*. The poem *Ode to Joy* expresses Schiller's (1775) idealistic vision of the human race becoming brothers — this was a vision shared by Beethoven. There are no words to this anthem; there is only the music — music is the universal language — the anthem expresses the European ideals of freedom, peace and solidarity.

Mindful awareness cultivates values within me, believing we are all equal and I need to have constant awareness of walls created within my mind that prevent me from reaching out to my fellow humans.

I often listen to Beethoven's *Ode to Joy*; the music is certainly calming, relaxing and inspirational.

Mindfulness Unlocked by Francis O' Toole

76. Friendship

"In the end, just three things matter: how well we have lived, how well we have loved, how well we have learned to let go." — Jack Kornfield

A girl came to ask the Oracle Rhema to discuss friendship and how demanding it can be at times.

She asked the Oracle Rhema, *"How can I best develop friendship?"* The Oracle Rhema responded, *"Friendship is a great gift to treasure but not take for granted. Yet, we must remember that true friendship is not all about giving. Friends must be willing to give as they receive. If your friends take more from you than you give, maybe they are not true friends."*

The Oracle Rhema continued, *"Unconditional friendship is when you don't mind giving and you don't expect anything in return because you care about them."*

Mindfulness encourages me to develop good positive relationships and friendships because they have a positive impact on my wellbeing. Mindful awareness will highlight that some relationships can be toxic and it's important to recognise this — we need to speak up if taken advantage of by others. If a relationship is causing a negative impact on my life, then I need to bring this negative relationship or friendship to an end.

I have found that difficulties between friends can easily be resolved if both are willing to talk and express concerns honestly. This can often lead to strengthening the bond of friendship. I was asked by a group of students in school to define friendship. I found it challenging to come up with an answer but gave the following response: *"Friendship is about respect; one speaks, the other listens."*

1. What is the quality of your friendships?

2. Are some of your friendships too demanding?

3. How much effort do you put into developing deeper friendships?

77. Empathy

"Life is a dance. Mindfulness is witnessing that dance."
— Amit Ray

A group of men gathered regularly in the local woods. They found a quiet place surrounded by trees, gathered some logs and lit a fire. They then sat in a circle around the fire and shared their experiences of life. They spoke at length about their achievements and failures. The philosophy behind this idea was that, by sharing their stories, each man could learn from the experience of others.

One night they invited the Oracle Rhema, curious to see whether she would offer any advice on how they could be enlightened. The Oracle Rhema listened to each man telling of his achievements, fears and weaknesses. After much talking and sharing, the men turned to the Oracle Rhema to have the final say. She too offered her advice, *"Men listen with deaf ears if they fail to show empathy, acceptance and love."*

Carl Rogers (1902–1987) was an American psychologist and one of the leading founders of the humanistic approach to psychology. When I was studying psychotherapy, Carl Rogers was presented as one of the founding fathers of psychotherapy. He spoke about the importance of a good relationship between the client and counsellor for a therapeutic session to be successful. The bond between both was really important; the client needs to know that the therapist is real and genuine. He thought that listening with empathy would bring about positive change in the individual during a counselling session.

Empathy is a psychological process to put oneself in the mental shoes of another to understand their pain, hurts, thoughts and emotions. When we do this, the person listening can often experience similar pain like that of the person who is sharing. This can bring great healing for both the giver and receiver.

The opposite is also true, if the giver shares painful insights about their personal life but finds the listener lacking in empathy — this can be dangerous and have a serious psychological consequences for the giver.

Mindful empathy continues to invite me to focus on how I am present to the other person. An important part of empathy for me is to have an awareness of my own feelings before trying to understand others; I try to put myself into another person's position and think about how they feel. With empathy, I am able to think about how others are treated or feel their pain. Empathy enables me to help, support and to reach out to them. This may mean listening to their thoughts or giving a hug. I need to have constant mindful awareness when I want to empathise with another person.

78. Sickness

"Peace comes from within. Do not seek it without."
— Buddha

The Oracle Rhema was seen as one who cared for the sick and dying, since she was spotted on many occasions visiting hospitals and attending to patients.

On one such occasion a nurse decided to ask her about the reasons for sickness. She approached the Oracle Rhema and asked, *"Why is there so much sickness in the world? Just look around and see some of our etiolated patients who need palliative care and some are even born with disabilities, like the young boy who has no arms or legs."*

After a moment of silence, the Oracle Rhema responded, *"I have no answers for physical evil like sickness but when I look around this ward I do experience love, kindness and care. I can see into hearts of the patients; they are full of gratitude for doctors, nurses and hospital staff."*

A few years ago, I was diagnosed with pernicious anaemia — a condition where I don't have enough healthy red blood cells to carry adequate oxygen throughout my body. The signs and symptoms for me are tiredness, muscle and bone pain. When I was diagnosed with this condition, I became angry with myself and life — as far as I was concerned, I did not deserve this. Through the practice of mindfulness, I became aware of the need to embrace my condition and not fight against it. I now have full awareness of my condition and limitations. I have to visit my GP every two months for an injection of Neo-Cytamen — this is given to patients with vitamin B12 deficiency. I really value all medical professionals for their skill, care and professionalism in working with people who are sick. Having a sense of humour can also help to embrace difficult situations — I laugh out loud on my regular visits to the doctor, seeing it as getting my 'jungle juice' to give me strength for another few weeks to face the challenges of life. There is a great deal of scientific research to show that mindfulness can help people who experience sickness on a journey to healing.

Mindfulness invites me to live with the questions even when I don't have all the answers. Through mindfulness I am gaining the strength to deal with my weaknesses.

Mindfulness Unlocked by Francis O' Toole

79. Self Care

"Relaxation means releasing all concern and tension and letting the natural order of life flow through one's being." — Donald Curtis

As a therapist working in the counselling profession for the last twenty years, most of my day involves listening to people. It is my role to be there for the client, listening to their needs and concerns, giving them time. With the client sharing as I listen, I look at the pattern in their behaviour or in the way they are thinking in order to gain an understanding of the person's life. My job is to identify the negative patterns and explore new ways of doing things that will give them key steps to follow, changing the way they think and feel, which will empower the person to have a better quality of life.

Over the years, I have identified one common pattern that many clients have in common, the need for 'self care'. It's amazing the amount of people who feel guilty on hearing the phrase 'self care' — The mum who is always there for her children, the employer who wants to care for his employees, the student who will not sacrifice time from his/her studies to have fun.

I believe the first duty each of us has is the duty to care for ourselves; to look after our health, our mind and bodies in a proactive way. This is the first responsibility we have to ourselves. No one else is responsible for our 'self care'. I often wonder, if we really cared for ourselves, would we have less people attending hospital for long-term illness? This is only a reflective question but there are many diseases that can be prevented if we care for ourselves.

How many people attend hospital with diseases that are related to diet, smoking, alcohol, stress, etc.? If we are honest, we all know that a healthier lifestyle will benefit our body, as well as our emotional and mental health.

I have made it a part of my life to try to eat well and stay away from substances that will affect my mind and body. For me, that relates to not drinking alcohol above recommended limits; for others it may be to say *"No"* to drugs or smoking. We all know what our weaknesses are, however, the purpose of this exercise is not to make one feel guilty but rather to help each of us focus on one area in our life that we want to improve.

I found that good 'self-care' will certainly help to build up my immune system, allowing me to feel good, and avoid sickness and disease while improving my wellbeing.

I invite you to make a list of three things in each of the following categories you are going to do to practise 'self care':

- Physical exercise

- Healthy food

- Relaxing time

- Having fun time

- Connecting with others

- Hobbies or interests

Mindfulness Unlocked by Francis O' Toole

80. Social Justice

"If we learn to open our hearts, anyone, including the people who drive us crazy, can be our teachers."
— Pema Chodron

Hundreds of people gathered at City Hall to discuss issues of social justice. They asked the Oracle Rhema for her views on social justice. She said, *"Before we discuss social justice, we have to understand poverty."*

"Poverty is the heart that cannot share,

The eyes that cannot see,

The hand that cannot give,

The ears that cannot listen,

The voice that cannot speak."

Mindfulness invites me to have an awareness of my basic senses: sight, hearing, smell, taste and touch. The sensing organs associated with the senses will send messages to our brain to help make sense and understand the world we perceive and experience.

I can choose to use my senses to understand the needs of all people in my local community, knowing that when I use my talents to support others, I end up having a warm feeling of gratitude and a good sense of wellbeing.

In Washington DC, there is a memorial in honour of Martin Luther King Jr. He is seen as the great freedom fighter for African Americans. I love his passion and vision of social justice for all. In 1963, in his famous speech for jobs and freedom, he said, *"The ultimate measure of a man is not where he stands in moments of comfort and convenience, but where he stands at times of challenge and controversy."* I had the privilege of standing on this very same spot where he made his famous speech at the Lincoln Memorial. Carved into the ground are Martin Luther King Jr.'s famous words *"I have a dream"*.

His vision was for democracy to become a reality for all people. I could sense the presence of great people like Martin Luther King Jr. and many great American presidents who stood at this spot. Mindful awareness keeps me in touch with my social conscience, which is inviting me to stand on the side of justice, peace and reconciliation.

Mindfulness Unlocked by Francis O' Toole

81. Ethos

"There's only one reason why you're not experiencing bliss at this present moment, and it's because you're thinking or focusing on what you don't have...but right now you have everything you need to be in bliss."
— Anthony de Mello

The pedantic headmaster of the academy was very proud of his control of both staff and students. There seemed to be good discipline in the academy and everyone followed the timetable with no one diverting from the system put in place. At the end of the academic year, the headmaster went to visit the Oracle Rhema seeking advice on other ways to improve the high standard set in the academy. The Oracle Rhema was keen to listen to all that the headmaster wanted to share about his academy. The headmaster informed the Oracle Rhema about how he had great plans and policies in place, in fact he ticked all the boxes concerning how an academy should be run. The Oracle Rhema looked for clarification: *"Was this a military or academic academy?"* To which the headmaster responded, *"An academic academy."* The Oracle Rhema responded, "Now *you need to dance with the students and observe how their spirit comes alive with music, laughter and fun."*

Mindfulness reminds me to have awareness when working or dealing with people that I connect with through social interaction. But if the focus of an institution is about ticking boxes — micro management only — then there is a real danger it will fail to touch the soul of the people who work or study there.

Mindfulness has taught me if I lose touch, the danger is that I will possibly lose sight of the purpose and philosophy of the founding members of the institution.

Mindfulness Unlocked by Francis O' Toole

82. Little Moments

"I think togetherness is a very important ingredient to family life." — Barbara Bush

At a parent conference the Oracle Rhema could hear the guidelines being given to parents to follow as best practice when dealing with their children. During the conference, the parents were real and honest when sharing their ideals and frustrations experienced in dealing with young people. The parents wanted the *'best'* for their sons and daughters: they wanted the *'best'* education, religion and extracurricular activities.

The parents always turned to the Oracle Rhema when in doubt and this occasion was no different. The parents asked the Oracle Rhema a straightforward question, *"What are the best gifts to give our children?"* The Oracle Rhema responded, *"The first gift is curiosity. Be willing to sit at the bedside of your child night after night listening to their questions. These questions will be the keys to opening their imagination and creativity. The second best gift is to teach the children how to read. This will allow them to develop their inner self and value the world around them in awe and wonder."*

The Oracle Rhema continued, *"With both of these gifts, they will be able to explore and research knowledge that will empower them to make the right choice and right decision."*

The greatest gift I received in life is the privilege to be a parent caring for my young children. I encourage them to develop the skill of curiosity and the ability to ask questions.

This skill empowers them to be able to look at issues from every perspective before making decisions and choices in life.

Now that my children are teenagers, I find time for shared activity — these fun moments allow us to explore the world around us. There are so many activities we can do with teenagers, ranging from cycling, mountain climbing, attending concerts, travel, etc. I ask my teenagers for assistance to make an endless list of possible activities.

Mindful awareness allows me to see the importance of engaging and being present to my children in the moment. Parents are constantly doing things to ensure their children have the '*best*' life can offer; mindfulness reminds me of the importance of connection and engaging through fun activities.

I need to be mindful that I am not disconnecting from my family life as a result of the difficulties and distractions I face in modern day society; for example, busy schedules, long commutes and social media.

If I have created a mindful bonding experience with my children, this will give them stability and allow them to connect maturely with society as they get older. It will also have the positive effect of building long-lasting relationships within the family.

The mindful attention in shared activities and time given to my children may be the best gift in life I can give them.

83. Calmness

"Treat everyone you meet as if they were you."
— Doug Dillon

To the amazement of the community, it seemed that the Oracle Rhema was always calm, at peace with herself and never lost her patience.

One day a member of the community wanted to know her secret and so he put this question to the Oracle Rhema: *"How can we control our emotions and have the right balance?"*

The Oracle Rhema replied, *"I live each day fully alive, make the best out of all the experiences life has to offer and never get stuck in the negative. This leaves my mind at peace with no distractions."*

I am reminded of the motivational poster produced during World War Two by the British Government to help the public to keep morale high, knowing they were going to experience a massive attack: *"Keep Calm and Carry On."*

Mindfulness reminds me that I will experience daily challenges in life: some positive, some negative; some will bring destruction while others will bring peace and happiness. Having good mindful awareness of my feelings, emotions and thinking will help me approach all challenges with strength. I allow the motivation poster to become part of my daily mindfulness: *"Keep Calm and Carry On."*

Mindfulness Unlocked by Francis O' Toole

84. Mantra

"Whatever the present moment contains, accept it as if you had chosen it. Always work with it, not against it."
— Eckhart Tolle

The Oracle Rhema was seen in a transfixed state under a tree repeating the message: *"I am loving, people love me."*

The locals who gathered had an impetuous desire to know what the Oracle Rhema was up to.

They summoned up the courage to ask the Oracle Rhema, *"Why are you repeating this mantra over and over?"* to which the Oracle Rhema responded, *"If I speak the mantra out loud, my ears will hear this beautiful message: 'I am loving and people love me.'"*

The Oracle Rhema then instructed the locals to, *"Listen carefully to those beautiful words, allow growth on your inward journey. Observe yourself chanting the mantra: 'I am loving, people love me.' Notice your heart with every citation experiencing peace and tremendous feelings of love."*

Mindfulness is inviting me to love myself before I can love others. I make choices every day to care for myself from what I decide to eat to how I am going to spend my time. It is important to have mindful awareness of my actions and observe whether they are positively enhancing my life.

In showing love to others, I reach out with the same care and respect that I show to myself. It is not my responsibility to change how others think or feel but it's my responsibility to always respect differences.

I find that keeping in touch with family and friends can be very rewarding as it leaves me having a good sense of wellbeing. Sometimes it may be difficult to physically meet people when the time suits me but then I know there are so many ways to contact those who are close and important to me, e.g. phone, email, social media, text, Facebook, Instagram, Twitter, etc. There is no excuse for not connecting.

In conclusion, mindfulness is reminding me firstly to believe, *"I am loving and people love me"* and secondly, *"Observe how well I keep connecting with others."*

85. Be Attentive

"Patience has all the time it needs." — Allan Lokos

The act of simple mindful listening is to be attentive, having the ability to hear conversations without adding any judgements or labels; it is the ability to hear exactly what is said at that moment. This is a great skill to have and one we all could develop easily.

I have often found myself listening to the radio in the car on my way home from work but find it difficult to recall what I heard when I eventually get home. It is the same when I listen to conversations: there is a danger I may not hear what is being said. Psychologists say we only hear 25% of what is said in normal — and not so normal — conversations.

If I am to be honest, this may happen to me every single day at work or with the people I socialise with; I listen but find my mind is easily distracted, therefore not taking in the information from the conversation. To really hear what the radio show is telling me or to really hear what is said in conversations, I need to develop the skill of mindful listening.

In mindful listening, I am trying to develop the skill of listening with 100% attention to everything I hear.

I try to be aware of what others are saying while in conversation and I keep challenging myself to really listen to the conversation. When I create this awareness around mindful listening, I hear more and I recall more. It also allows me to be fully present to the other person, empathising and connecting.

When I listen to others or when others are listening to me, I feel a real connection with the other person. We will have better professional relationships with our colleagues as we will show that we are genuinely interested in what they are saying. Mindful listening will allow us to develop our knowledge base, as when we listen we gain more. It will help me develop my self confidence as I become more knowledgeable.

When I am not listened to, I feel disconnected and even alienated. I find that listening as a counsellor is crucial to my work — if I fail to listen then people will not return, creating a breakdown in communication and trust.

When I am listening to the other person mindfully, I hear every word that is spoken and clearly understand the message the other person wants to relate. This will also help develop my relationship with them, since they will see me as someone who genuinely cares and is interested in what they have to say.

I invite you to do the following exercise, which will help to develop the skill of listening mindfully.

1. Try to spend five minutes daily in silence. This will give your brain and ears a rest, allowing time for renewal to enable you to listen with acute sharpness when the need arises.

2. Listening to different sounds is a good exercise to practise, for example when listening to music, try to identify different instruments in a band and hear the sounds that are most appealing to you. I know I like to listen to Jazz music because I find it calming and relaxing. Somewhere in my mind I have given myself this message. My emotions have an influence on how well I listen. This reminds me that when listening to

Mindfulness Unlocked by Francis O' Toole

people I may have created certain emotional judgments, either negative or positive, about this person which will impact on my ability to really listen. I need to be aware of how my emotions affect my listening.

3. When out in nature, listen to all the sounds around you: running water in a river, the wind howling or leaves on a tree, the musical sound of birds or animals creating their different sounds. This exercise will also help to improve the quality of your listening skills.

4. When listening as part of a conversation, become aware of eye contact and body movement showing how well you consciously listen. This will enable you to receive the information by paying attention to the other person. When you ask questions to clarify, you are connected to the person and the conversation.

5. Watch out for distractions. If you are multi-tasking it is not possible to listen fully e.g. engaging on social media and trying to listen to others at the same time.

6. Enter conversations as if you really want to learn something new and listen as if this conversation is really important.

7. Stay focused on the conversation and show that you really care about what is being said.

8. The average person speaks about two hundred and twenty-five words per minute. You need to listen with the intent to understand or you could switch off and catch only seventy-five words.

Mindful listening allows our ears, mind and heart to be open in a non-judgemental way, allowing us to hear sounds with clarity in the present moment.

Mindfulness Unlocked by Francis O' Toole

86. Praise

"Begin at once to live and count each separate day as a separate life." — Seneca

The Oracle Rhema was invited to attend a graduation at the end of the school term for students. On this day each student received their scroll in recognition of graduation and many received awards for achievements in the area of academics, sports and music. The Oracle Rhema was asked to speak. She stood at the podium and acknowledged the achievements of the young students. She went on to say, *"Firstly, it is important to give ourselves recognition, praise and to acknowledge the positive qualities we all have. Secondly, when we get public recognition, we know that we did a good job."*

Mindfulness allows me to dig deep and recognise that real success comes when I can see that my efforts and hard work are really worth it, even if I receive no public reward. I need to strive for an internal focus of evaluation — this is better for my mental health and stops me looking for approval from others.

Through mindfulness I understand that positive self belief is important to help me face challenges with resilience and adversity with strength.

I invite you to ask yourself: how do you manage to celebrate your success and that of others?

Mindfulness Unlocked by Francis O' Toole

87. Poverty

"The way is not in the sky, the way is in the heart."
— Buddha

A man came to the Oracle Rhema asking about the existence of poverty in the world and whether it was possible to prevent it.

The Oracle Rhema responded by telling a Zen story about a blind beggar who continued to sit on a public street with an empty bowl beside him. People passed by and said nothing, nor did they put anything into the bowl. A young girl was walking by. She had no money but was upset looking at the blind beggar and wondered what she could do to help. She went home, got a pen, colouring crayons and a large sheet of paper. She came back to the blind beggar, sat beside him, wrote on a sheet of paper with beautiful colourful writing and placed her poster beside him. Now people stopped as they passed by and placed money into the bowl. The blind man was unsure what was happening and so stopped one person and asked, *"What is written on the sheet of paper?"* The stranger replied, *"It is a beautiful day. You can see it. I cannot."*

The Oracle Rhema went on to say, *"Thoughts and words create a positive or negative effect on others. When using the right words, we can connect and help others."*

Mindful awareness helps me to cultivate my insight, allowing my mind and heart to grow in love, care and respect for all people.

Mindfulness Unlocked by Francis O' Toole

88. Loving Kindness

"Don't let life harden your heart." — Pema Chodron

A woman went to the Oracle Rhema seeking advice: *"How best can I support my colleague at work who seems to be under a lot of pressure and stress?"* The Oracle Rhema responded, *"Be yourself and take time to be with the other person while continuing to listen to their problems."*

Mindfulness is inviting me to reach out and care for other people, remembering that my first duty is to care for myself before I can care for others.

Many scholars, philosophers, artists, writers, poets, Theologians and songwriters have often written about the power of the word 'Love'. The word love could be defined as a strong feeling of affection one person has for another. We can all recognise the love a parent has for his/ her young baby or the love adults experience in relationships with each other. Love is often seen to have a huge positive impact on our brain and wellbeing. Love is also seen as an important attribute for mindfulness; in fact, I would suggest it is absolutely essential and makes mindfulness palatable and attractive for all ages.

'Loving-kindness' is a most important exercise to practise for mindfulness. It is highly commendable to practise daily self care and love of others. It is like planting a seed that will grow and bring love to others whom we meet daily in our lives.

When I allow my heart to experience love, this creates a passion like a fire that will want to spread quickly among those around us. The love within will create a new energy flow that wants to burst with life. If my heart is smiling, all of my body will smile, releasing tension, hatred and anxiety.

I will share love intentionally and unintentionally, attracting the same energy from those around me. Love will allow me to become a beacon of hope and the greatest exponent of a simple idea the world is hungry for.

I have found the daily practice of 'loving kindness' energising, exciting and uplifting. I invite you to take time daily to practise 'loving kindness'.

Let's try the following exercises, which could last for five to twenty minutes:

STAGE ONE

Begin with the breath, taking three deep breaths, watching the rise and fall of your chest. When you feel relaxed and ready, recite inwardly the following:

"May I be filled with 'loving kindness';

May I have peace of mind and heart;

May I be safe from inner and outer dangers;

May I be at ease and be happy;

May I be filled with 'loving kindness'."

Repeat the above phrase three or four times while keeping a gentle smile on your face.

STAGE TWO

This time, replace the word 'I' with the name of a person you love, this could be your partner or child.

Mindfulness Unlocked by Francis O' Toole

Begin with the breath, taking three deep breaths, watching the rise and fall of your chest. When you feel relaxed and ready, recite inwardly the following:

"May (name of loved one) be filled with 'loving kindness';

May (name of loved one) have peace of mind and heart;

May (name of loved one) be safe from inner and outer dangers;

May (name of loved one) be at ease and be happy;

May (name of loved one) be filled with 'loving-kindness'."

Repeat the above phrase three or four times while keeping a gentle smile on your face.

When you practise this exercise of 'loving kindness', watch for the warm sensations and love within all of your body. This meditation could be practised once a day or once a week. I have found deep love in my heart each time I have practised this exercise. I am also reminded of the love and goodness in other people.

It is also important to be aware that the 'loving kindness' exercise can bring up feelings of hurt, pain and brokenness which are deeply rooted in the history of our lives, reminding us of a relationship that did not go according to plan. If this happens, it is so important to be gentle, kind and patient with ourselves and even allow more time for loving kindness.

This 'loving kindness' exercise is full of unconditional love towards myself and towards other people I care for. As I practise this exercise, I increasingly create awareness around me of the love, warmth and peace that can be achieved within. When I allow myself to be filled with the energy of loving kindness, a kind smile radiates within my heart, which is clearly seen on my face, bringing peace, security and love to those I meet.

89. Power of Silence

"The tree of silence bears the fruit of peace"
— Arabian Proverbs

Parents and medical professionals who have the privilege of witnessing the birth of a child will speak about the incredible experience of watching a baby leaving the comfort of the womb for the challenge it will face in the world. The first major challenge will be the collapse and cutting of the umbilical cord which is still connected to the mum supplying oxygen and blood: when this happens the baby will survive independently.

This moment of birth is a very sacred moment; the beginning of a new life. Those who are present for births will tell you that there is a deep powerful silence as we wait intensely to hear the child take his/her first breath. Somewhere deep in our being we know there are unwritten rules telling us not to speak at this time, not to make noise, just to be silent. The very moment belongs to the new child entering into the world. This is also a moment when — rightfully — care, respect and medical attention is given to the mother of the child. In silence and with a first breath, a new life is born, bringing joy to those who gather.

It is so easy for me to experience and feel that first breath in the gift and power of silence as I listen to my in breath (inhale) and listen to my out breath (exhale). The power of silence is held at that moment after inhale; I hold it for a second or two before the exhale of breath. This 'before moment' is so powerful: it is when the soul enriches our body and mind, bringing renewal, energy and life. The soul demands silence in the body as it captures that moment before the exhale of breath, allowing for the gentle flow of renewal.

It could also be compared to the dawn chorus in the morning; just as the pregnant darkness leaves the world and gives birth to daylight, there is a moment of stillness and powerful silence. Then at the birth of a new day, the dawn chorus breaks out: the birds sing and welcome the start of a new day.

I often walk along the banks of the river Boyne for hours listening to the sounds of nature and enjoying the beauty the river has to offer as it blends with the landscape covered with trees. It is only in the power of silence without headphones or social media can I hear and see the awesome beauty and colours of nature.

Along the banks of the Boyne you will come across Slane Castle, which was built in the 1780s by the Conyngham family and hosted King George IV. Today, this castle is used for concerts, weddings, special events and even has a new distillery producing the world famous Slane whiskey. It is here that I encountered the hermitage of St. Erc who died in 514 A.D. on the grounds of Slane Castle.

It is said he was a pagan druid and the only member of King Laoghaire, who became a follower of St. Patrick. After his conversion to Christianity he was appointed the first Bishop of Slane, taking on the new mission to preach and teach the gospel of Christ to the people of Munster.

After his retirement he returned to Slane, lived out the rest of his life in silence, meditation and complete solitude at this hermitage beside the Boyne until his death at the age of 93. For me this hermitage has a wonderful history and a

Mindfulness Unlocked by Francis O' Toole

reminder of great people like St. Erc who continue to challenge us to listen to the power of silence.

If this silence cannot be found in your busy routine of life or in your environment, then go into the woods, forests or fields and be at one with nature. If you get the opportunity, seek out the sacred hermitage place of St. Erc hidden beneath the trees on the Boyne. Here the light will shine through the outstretched branches of the trees, guiding you on a path and illuminating the relics of this sacred ancient ruins. This place is kept secret by the trees' protection and illuminating the relics of this sacred ancient ruins.

Mindfulness and spiritual growth can only be gained in the power of silence. I do not have to live a life in total silence or live the life of a monk like St. Erc to achieve this silence but I can find moments daily to be in touch with the power of silence within my heart.

There are many public places where our culture and society will demand silence, for example, churches, graveyards, sacred places, a library, etc. I am often reminded of the power of silence at public meetings or at major sporting games like the GAA where thousands may be gathered in Croke Park and there is a call for one minutes' silence to mark the death of a famous person or in remembrance of a tragic event in the course of history. This is what I would call a cultural silence, which is a large group of people sharing in the collective power of silence.

I know that silence has a place in our society. I know that people have retreated — and will continue to retreat — from the world to be silent. I know that people go on long journeys to find this silence, like the climbing of Croagh

Patrick or travelling on long journeys to walk the Camino in Spain.

The greatest power of silence of all is found at the moment of death. On many occasions I have attended to family, friends and neighbours during their final hours where all are gathered in silence or a gentle whisper. This moment of silence is in respect of the person in their last hours awaiting the ultimate moment of final breath.

Mindfulness builds courage and strength within, enabling me to be comfortable and at ease with the 'power of silence'. This will allow me to experience life and death in all its fullness.

90. Mindfulness In Traffic

"We are made wise not by the recollection of our past, but by the responsibility for our future."
— George Bernard Shaw

It can be very frustrating when caught in traffic for a very long period. This was my experience for a number of years as I commuted to Dublin city for work only to spend three hours daily in heavy traffic. I can only empathise with those who have to begin their working day stuck in traffic. I have often had an appointment but left it a bit late to get there, ending up frustrated when stuck in traffic, worried about missing my appointment. Regularly I see others in their cars expressing anger and annoyance when delayed by heavy traffic. When people are really annoyed they express this by blowing the horn in the car or using bad language. One day I experienced an ugly scene in Dublin city rush hour when two men got out of their cars and began a fist fight. Road rage is not acceptable.

I found it possible to reduce stress during my morning and evening commute with mindfulness awareness while driving. When driving I am particularly mindful and focus my mind on health and safety especially going on a long journey. I make a conscious decision not to allow the actions of others dictate how I feel. On most occasions there is nothing I can do only accept the traffic for what it is. When driving I made a conscious decision to work with my emotions, allowing me to pay attention to the present moment.

I invite you to use the following mindfulness exercise when driving:

Always be prepared before leaving on a long car journey. This will save you from distractions about something you may have left behind. Consciously become aware of the journey ahead and how you are feeling before you even put on your safety belt.

When driving take deep breaths, allowing for balance to come back into your life, freeing you from stress. This reminds you to drive with care.

Tune into some classical music, which will help keep you calm and relaxed. Always avoid phone calls or texting while driving.

It is good to observe all that is happening around you while driving. Then become consciously aware observing the feelings in your body. How are your hands on the steering wheel? Become aware of your upper back against the seat. Is there tension or do you feel relaxed? Is there tension in your neck? Can you feel the vibration of the engine on the pedals? A simple body scan is a good idea to assess whether you are relaxed or driving in a state of tension.

Keep your eyes on the road. Check your speed and mirror regularly. Notice your surroundings: the weather, road conditions, the amount of traffic on the road — do this while observing the rules of the road. Notice the cars behind you and in front of you. Notice if you are having thoughts and feelings about the current situation that may be a distraction. Allow for them but keep coming back to your main focus of driving safely. This type of mindful awareness is allowing you to give full attention to the present moment, staying safe as you drive.

Mindfulness Unlocked by Francis O' Toole

If you are very tired and feeling sleepy, it is highly recommended not to go on a long journey or to take regular breaks on the way. It is a good idea to have a bottle of fresh water in the car especially when you are embarking on a long journey. Best be prepared and always plan the route of your journey before taking off.

Finally, you could practise loving kindness by repeating the following silently or out loud: *"May I be filled with love and kindness. May I be happy. May I be at peace. May I be safe as I drive."* You could repeat this loving kindness exercise and replace *"I"* with *" all drivers"*, for example, *"May all drivers be safe as they drive."* The practice of loving kindness while driving will allow you to have a good sense of wellbeing. It will also allow you to empathise and be patient with other drivers.

Using the skill of mindfulness while commuting allows me to become more calm and relaxed, arriving at my workplace feeling refreshed and ready for work. It is the same after a long day at work, driving home mindfully allows me to recharge, ready to have an enjoyable and relaxing evening.

Since having awareness of mindfulness while driving, I became more aware of the amount of cars on the road and the amount of people driving alone like myself. I now travel where and when possible using public transport. This has given me many more benefits than driving alone: I don't have to worry about finding a parking space; it can be an opportunity to chat with people or just be silent; it is certainly less stressful; it can be faster when a bus can use bus lanes in city traffic; using a city tram or train can get me to a region directly without having to negotiate other traffic users; public transport users use significantly less air pollution per passenger mile than a standard car with only a driver and no passengers. The next best benefit for me using public transport is the extra time I gain: I can read a book, attend to social media, make a phone call, or sit back and relax.

Mindfulness Unlocked by Francis O' Toole

91. Mindful Walking

"Every path, every street in the world is your walking meditation path." — Thich Nhat Hanh

'Mindful walking' is the most convenient form of mindfulness exercise because you don't need any special equipment. There is no preparation involved and it is probably the easiest form of exercise to take. During my walks I will breathe steadily and clearly; as a result of this steady movement, I only have to listen to the sound of my breath.

I aim to complete 10,000 steps daily at least five times a week using a free app on my mobile phone as a guide. I truly enjoy this walk; I find it refreshing and energising. I also like the idea of 10,000 steps since it sets a clear goal and target to be reached. A survey carried out in 2010 showed that walking has a whole host of positive benefits from improving cardiovascular health, decreasing stress and improving wellbeing. The American Heart Association claims that daily brisk walking can lower cholesterol and reduce the risk of heart disease and diabetes, thus improving the quality of our physical and mental health.

As I walk mindfully, I take the time to admire the beauty of nature. I watch for as many different colours as possible that I spot on birds, animals, trees and plants. It never ceases to amaze me how many different shades of green exist and how lots of creatures have adapted to their green environment by taking on a green hue themselves as camouflage.

I look at the trees to seek out the tallest tree and try to spot as many different types of trees can I see in any one day. I find trees a great example in mindfulness because they don't move but grow tall and straight reaching for the sky. They are constant in their state of breathing in and breathing out. In winter time they stand tall, naked and beautiful, bending with the winds and harsh conditions. In summer they are colourful giving life and shelter to birds, insects along with so many different animals. The trees are open to challenging weather conditions while remaining deeply rooted in the place where they were planted or given life.

It is not surprising that in ancient Celtic tradition the people believe that the trees represented mother earth allowing life to be given to humans and when they die, their soul returns to the trees. The Bible tells of the story of creation where Adam and Eve meet at the apple tree. Many Greek philosophers are described gaining insight when sitting under a tree for example the Tree of Hippocrates, this could be said of scientist like Newton the mathematician, astronomer and theologian. Even great religious leaders, for example the Buddha gained insight while under a tree. The tree has a special meaning and understanding for lots of people throughout the ages. The next time you are out walking, touch the bark of the tree feeling its strength and admire its beauty.

'Mindful walking' helps me to unwind from the busy daily routine of life. It allows me to be in touch with nature creating space in my mind to be open to inspiration. *'Mindful walking'* allows me to see the beauty, awe and wonders of nature and be filled with gratitude for the gift of life.

Mindfulness Unlocked by Francis O' Toole

92. Laughter

"If you concentrate on finding whatever is good in every situation, you will discover that your life will suddenly be filled with gratitude, a feeling that nurtures the soul."
— Rabbi Harold Kushner

The Oracle Rhema attended a conference with leaders of education. From the moment she walked into the large room, she was aware of the distinguished guests and very experienced people. Everyone was ready to make their presentation. The Oracle Rhema wondered about the institution each individual was responsible for and their style of leadership? When it was time for the Oracle Rhema to speak, she decided to present a different topic at the last second. *"Let's talk about laughter,"* she said. With that, people began laughing, thinking it was a good starting line for a presentation to begin with a joke. The Oracle Rhema continued, *"We often forget about one of the best tools we all have when faced with a difficult situation: the gift of Laughter."*

Mindfulness teaches me that having awareness of laughter and how I use this wonderful free gift can help to reduce stress and anxiety, and this allows me to relax. People who use laughter often seem to be more confident and certainly don't have stress written across their faces. Scientists tell us that laughter helps us to cope with difficult situations by suppressing the stress-related hormones in the brain. Laugher also releases brain chemicals called endorphins, the body's natural pain relievers, which give us that warm, fuzzy feeling of wellbeing.

So, laughter not only allows us to have fun with family, friends and at work, it may really be the best medicine!

Using laughter as a tool helps me to relax at work, before an interview or before I give a presentation. This is the perfect solution to reduce stress. It is said that it takes forty-three muscles to frown but only seventeen to smile. Smiling relaxes the muscles in our face.

My motto: *"Keep smiling, its free."*

Observe how many times you laugh today!

93. Laughter Yoga

"Between stimulus and response there is a space.
In that space is our power to choose our response.
In our response lies our growth and freedom."
— Viktor Frankl

I came across the idea of 'laughter yoga' only recently when reading the work developed by Indian physician Madan Kataria, who writes about the practice in his book *Laugh For No Reason*. He claims that 'laughter yoga' aids in the prevention of depression, anxiety and psychosomatic disorders. I have since tried this exercise on many occasions myself, with students in school and with personnel in large corporate companies when facilitating workshops on mindfulness. 'Laughter yoga' is based on the belief that voluntary laughter provides the same positive physiological and psychological benefits as spontaneous laughter to a joke or humorous event. I practise this exercise regularly, regardless of my emotional state — whether I'm feeling high or low or under stress. I found 'laughter yoga' certainly leaves me feeling good, more relaxed and tension free. I have no doubt it helps to reduce stress and improves health, self-confidence and wellbeing.

When doing 'laughter yoga', I do not need jokes or something funny to make me laugh. You might say I am faking the laugh but the mind does not know this.

Like all mindful exercise, I begin with awareness of breath and awareness of body. I will start with a warm up exercise to include stretching, eye contact with my body and clapping of hands. The warm up exercises will help break down inhibitions and allow us to be open to having fun.

I will laugh, laugh and laugh for about thirty seconds followed by silence for thirty seconds. I repeat this exercise over and over for periods of five or ten minutes.

I invite you to use this exercise daily of 'laughter yoga' to develop positive outcomes in your life. I found that the daily 'laughter yoga' allows me to shake off the negative attitudes and bring on positive vibes. If we use this powerful emotion, it has the ability to change us for the better and also our community to make the world a more peaceful and positive place to be.

'Laughter yoga' is practised in many countries and now has a set day on the calendar year — the first Sunday in May to celebrate World Laughter Day.

Once you have developed the skills of 'laughter yoga', progress to 'shaking yoga'. 'Shaking yoga' is about healing ourselves by shaking and vibrating the body as much as possible, achieving freedom from stress. Shake and vibrate the body for thirty seconds followed by stillness for thirty seconds. I repeat this exercise over and over for periods of five to ten minutes. Try doing both 'laughter yoga' and 'shaking yoga' together — it's fun and both help with stress reduction.

Mindfulness Unlocked by Francis O' Toole

94. Poetry

"May my life flow like a river, ever surprised by its own unfolding." — John O'Donohue

I find writing poetry can be a great exercise in mindfulness and allows me to be present to the moment. The following poem I composed as I walked by the river Liffey in Dublin — it captures what was going on in my mind at that moment in time.

Liffey

Full of glitter,
With no litter,
Refreshes our city
North and south.

Two link pillars,
Academic giants,
Trinity on the south,
Belvedere on the north,
Preparing for a knowledge economy.

Liffey
Running deep,
Not a swimmer,
Willing to leap,
River flowing.

Glowing boardwalks,
Tourist gawk,
Homeless gather,
Sleeping bags in hand.

Some exchanges,
No change given.

O'Connell Bridge,
People cross
When church bells ring.

Wind blows,
High tides,
Boats float,
Low tides,
Blending with the wind,

Seagulls, grey or white
Are dynamite
With their squawking calls,
Webbed feet,
Scavenge opportunistically,
Food left by the colourful tourists.

With a helicopter glance,
How important to take a stance,
Smell the air,
Listen to the sounds,
Absolutely yes,
A place for romance.

Liffey,
Full of weakness,
Sorrowful stories,
Famine ships, coffin ships,
Merchant vessels,
Your secrets are safe,

While I awake.

Mindfulness Unlocked by Francis O' Toole

95. Who Am I?

"The essence of beauty is being without self-deception."
— Pema Chodron

A student of psychology was confused about his identity, because he was bullied in secondary school. He developed a false belief that there was something wrong with him and he would never be accepted by his peers. He was unhappy as he continued to battle with the question, *"Who Am I?"* He went to the Oracle Rhema seeking help, to understand the person he is and the person he was becoming. After talking to the Oracle Rhema for a very long time, the Oracle Rhema refused to give the young man the answer he wanted to hear; after all he was the psychologist.

The Oracle Rhema did make one suggestion to the student, requesting him to *"sit in silence and be still for five minutes daily for the next month."* When the student returned to the Oracle Rhema four weeks later, he was delighted to reveal that he followed the Oracle Rhema's instructions. But each time he felt he had an answer to a question, this would be immediately followed with another question.

The Oracle Rhema told the student that *"it takes time and practice to develop who we are at every moment in life but each moment will reveal another part of who we are."*

Many religious monks and priests in orders from Hinduism, Islam, Roman Catholicism, Judaism and Buddhism are required to wear a habit which is an outward sign and public expression of the life they have chosen. The habits generally stand for modesty, humility and a way of life.

Mindful awareness is inviting me to develop 'internal habits' comprising repeated daily practice which creates 'awareness' of breathing, being still, being present to the moment, caring for my mind, body and spirit. These internal habits will enable me to be real and authentic. It will give me the strength, courage and will, to free myself to focus on quality interaction with people and the environment I experience day by day. They will help me to understand the person 'I am'.

The psychologist Joseph Luft came up with the following theory called the 'Johari window'. This is a technique that enables people to better understand themselves and have an awareness of how they interact with others. It is to encourage self disclosure and an openness to constructive feedback as a way of discovering our true hidden self.

This is a simple and easy tool to work with as we focus on our personality. According to the 'Johari window', there are four parts to our personality.

Imagine a window frame with four equal parts.

The first frame represents a part of me that I know and no one else knows.

The second frame represents the part of me that I know and others see.

The third frame represents the part of me that others see but I can't.

The fourth frame represents the part of me that is the most exciting part — the part of me unknown by me and unknown to others. This part I have yet to discover.

Mindfulness Unlocked by Francis O' Toole

I am still learning and discovering more about myself. During my time as a student of philosophy and theology, I had a spiritual director who was there guiding and helping me to recognise myself in a way I would never have the courage to do. When training as a psychotherapist, I had to have a supervisor to guide me with my client work. I also had to be the client and go for personal counselling as part of my training for the masters of science in family therapy. Today, I still seek spiritual direction, look to my supervisor regarding counselling client work and attend for counselling myself. I see all of these professionals as mentors who are there to give support and encouragement to empower me to be able to tap into my inner resources. My mentors have taught me to move beyond fear and find the right pathway in life. The mentors invited me to see my inner hidden strengths and to open my heart and mind to all possibilities. They allowed me to find my own truth and goodwill within.

Thankfully, I had good mentors — and friends who also are mentors but may not be aware of how they guided me at different stages in my life. Mentoring is based on a special bond between two people based on care, respect and loyalty. Every good mentor will have a strict code of ethics and boundaries. I need to be able to trust and confide in them. Each mentor I had allowed me to grow, develop and come closer to understanding who I am. I also became a mentor to many adults over time and I am honoured to be a mentor to young people as their teacher and counsellor in school.

I invite you on that journey of mindfulness self-discovery to explore any part of you that has yet to reveal itself — if you never had a mentor, find one for yourself. A mentor can be one significant adult in your life, a friend, a therapist, a teacher or a wise colleague.

As part of the process in writing this book, I made a special journey to Athens, the capital of Greece. It was also the heart of Ancient Greece, a powerful empire. Here I experienced the layers of myth, culture, art, legends, war history but was inspired mostly with my visit to the Temple of Apollo and seat of the Oracle of Delphi. In Ancient Greece, 6th century BC politicians, military leaders and individuals came here from the entire known world to seek predictions about the future. Delphi is now a major tourist destination with over five hundred thousand visitors a year learning about the past.

Through writing *Mindfulness Unlocked*, I have gained a better understanding of myself. I am always learning on this journey of life and I learn so much from others. We all need to believe that everyone possesses insights and wisdom, like the Oracle Rhema, that can be unlocked to help us lead a mindful life where we can grow and flourish.

Mindfulness Unlocked by Francis O' Toole

QUOTES ARE TAKEN FROM:

Abraham Lincoln was the US President who preserved the union during the civil war in the United States and brought about the emancipation of slaves. He was assassinated in 1865 in Washington D.C.

Alan Cohen is an author of inspirational books, including the best-selling *'The Dragon Doesn't Live Here Anymore'*.

Albert Einstein's teachings had a major influence on the philosophy of science. He received the Nobel Prize in 1921 for his work in physics.

Albert Schweitzer received the Nobel Prize in 1952 for his philosophy of 'Reverence for life'.

Allan Lokos began his career as a professional singer before establishing the Community Meditation Centre, New York, USA. He has written many books and articles on caring for self with compassion and determination.

Amit Ray is an Indian author who writes extensively on meditation, spirituality and yoga.

Anais Nin is an author of short stories who wrote many personal reflections, which were published, about her relationships and sexual abuse by her father.

Anthony de Mello is an Indian Jesuit priest and psychotherapist who wrote about spirituality and awareness.

Arabian Proverbs

Aristotle is an ancient Greek philosopher and scientist who died in 322 B.C.

Barbara Bush was the first lady of the United States from 1989 to 1993. She was married to George H. W. Bush.

Benjamin Franklin was one of the founding fathers of the United States.

Brendan Kennelly is an Irish poet and novelist. Since his retirement from teaching, he has been titled 'Professor Emeritus' by Trinity College Dublin.

Brian Greene is an American theoretical physicist and mathematician.

Buddha a spiritual leader and sage on whose teachings Buddhism was founded.

Carl Jung was a psychiatrist and psychoanalyst who founded analytical psychology.

Carl Rogers is an American psychologist and founder of the humanistic approach to psychology, widely used in the area of counselling.

Carl Sagan is an American scientist, astronomer and author.

Charles R. Swindoll is an author and evangelical christian pastor.

Chinese Proverb

Dalai Lama is an important monk in the school of Tibetan Buddhism.

Dan Zadra is an author and inspirational speaker.

Donald Curtis is an actor best known for spellbound.

Doug Dillon is a former United States Secretary of the Treasury.

Eckhart Tolle is a spiritual leader and best known as the author of *'The Power Of Now'*.

Elena Stasik is Vice President of Operations at the Rejuvenation Operation Therapeutic Core.

Eric Schmidt is an American billionaire businessman and software engineer. He was executive chairman of Google 2001–2015.

Eugène Ionesco was a Romanian-French playwright.

Euripides (480–406 BC) was a tragedian of classical Athens.

Francis de Sales was a canonised saint with the Roman Catholic Church. His motto was, *"He who preaches with love, preachers effectively"*.

Frederick W. Robertson was an author and famous preacher in England.

George Bernard Shaw was an Irish playwright, critic, polemicist and political activist. In 1925 was awarded the Nobel Prize in Literature.

George Eliot (real name Mary Anne Evans) was an English poet, novelist and journalist.

Helen Keller was an author and political activist. She was the first deaf-blind person to receive a Bachelor of Arts degree.

Henry David Thoreau was an American essayist, philosopher and poet.

Howard Thurman died in 1981. He was an African-American civil rights leader, author, theologian and educator.

Jack Kornfield is a leading American teacher of Buddhism, who is influential in introducing mindfulness to the West.

Jan Chozen Bays is a Zen teacher, author and paediatrician specialising in work with abused children.

Janice Marturano is an author and mindfulness teacher.

Jayne Morris is an author, life coach and international inspirational speaker.

Johann Wolfgang von Goethe is a German writer and statesman.

John F. Kennedy was the 35th President of the United States, assassinated in 1963 in Dallas, Texas, USA.

John O'Donohue is an Irish author, priest, poet and philosopher who is best known for his book *'Anam Cara'*.

Jon Kabat-Zinn is the founding director of mindfulness-based stress reduction and the Centre for Mindfulness and Health Care at the University of Massachusetts Medical School, USA.

Joseph Campbell is an author and an American professor who worked in comparative mythology and comparative religion.

Les Brown is an American motivational speaker, author, radio and television host.

Lewis B. Smedes is an ethicist and theologian.

M. Scott Peck is an American psychiatrist best known for his book *'The Road Less Traveled'*.

Mark Williams and **Danny Penman** are both authors in the area of mindfulness.

Mahatma Gandhi was an Indian activist and the leader of independence for his people against British rule.

Marcel Proust was a French novelist and critic who died in 1922.

Marcus Aurelius was a Roman Emperor from 161 to 180 A.D. He was also a writer and philosopher.

Martin Luther King Jr. was an American Baptist Minister and civil rights leader, assassinated in 1968.

Matthieu Ricard is a Buddhist monk and French writer best known for his books on happiness and Altruism.

Mother Teresa is best known for her work with the poorest of the poor in Calcutta. She was awarded the Nobel Peace Prize and after her death was canonised a saint by the Roman Catholic Church.

Nelson Mandela was an anti-apartheid revolutionary, political leader and president of South Africa from 1991 to 1999. He died in 2013.

Nido Qubein is an American-Lebanese businessman and motivational speaker.

Oscar Wilde was an Irish poet and playwright.

Padraig O'Morain is an Irish psychotherapist who has written a number of books on mindfulness.

Pema Chodron is an American Tibetan Buddhist and teacher.

Plato was an ancient Greek philosopher and writer in classical Greece. He was a student of Socrates and mentor of Aristotle.

Rabbi Harold Kushner is an author and prominent rabbi in Judaism.

Raji Lukkoor is best known for her book *'Inner Kingdom'*.

Ralph Ellison is an American novelist, best known for his novel *'Invisible Man'*.

Rasheed Ogunlaru is an English writer and life coach.

Robert Goddard was an American professor and engineer. He is credited with building the world's first liquid-fuelled rocket. He died in 1945 in Baltimore, USA.

Robert Orben is an American author in the area of comedy.

Ruby Wax OBE is an American actress, author and mental health campaigner.

Rumi, who died in 1273, was a Muslim poet, scholar and theologian.

Samantha Power served as US Ambassador to the United Nations from 2013–2017. Author and currently a Professor of Practice at Harvard Law School and Harvard Kennedy School.

Seneca was a Roman philosopher who died in 65 A.D.

Sharon Salzberg is a teacher of Buddhist meditation and is a New York Times best-selling author.

Sheikh Zayed bin Sultan Al Nahyan is the late President and founder of the United Arab Emirates.

Socrates was a classical Greek philosopher who died in 399 B.C. He is credited as one of the founders of western philosophy. He did not write down his teachings; information about him came from his followers and those who knew of his work.

Sonia Ricotti is the author of '*The Law of Attraction*'.

Steve Jobs was an American entrepreneur. He was the chairman, chief executive officer and co-founder of Apple Inc.

Steven Harrison is the author of many books, including '*The Love of Uncertainty*' and '*The Happy Child*'.

Sylvia Boorstein is from California. She lectures on mindfulness and Buddhism.

Tara Brach is an American psychologist who lectures on Buddhism and meditation. She founded the Insight Meditation Community, Washington.

Terri Guillemets is a quotation anthologist and author from Phoenix, Arizona.

Theodore Rubin is an American psychiatrist and author.

Thich Nhat Hanh is a Vietnamese monk and peace activist. He lives in the Plum Village Meditation Centre in southwest France. He has written many books on meditation and mindfulness.

Thucydides died in 395 B.C.. He was an Athenian historian and general.

Turkish Proverbs

Ursula K Le Guin was an American novelist.

Viktor Frankl was an Austrian neurologist and psychiatrist as well as a holocaust survivor. He died in 1997.

Walt Whitman was an American poet, essayist and journalist.

Mindfulness Unlocked by Francis O' Toole

Index

If you enjoyed *Mindfulness Unlocked*, please post a review on Amazon and Goodreads.

Thank you for your custom!

Other titles by Francis O' Toole:

Walking On Air is available from Amazon.

Printed in Great Britain
by Amazon